GHOST
IN THE
MIRROR

GHOST
IN THE
MIRROR

Real Cases
of Spirit Encounters

Leslie Rule

Andrews McMeel
Publishing, LLC
Kansas City

08 09 10 11 12 MLT 10 9 8 7 6 5 4 3 2 1

Library of Congress Cataloging-in-Publication Data
Rule, Leslie, 1958–
    Ghost in the mirror : real cases of spirit encounters / Leslie Rule.
    p. cm.
    ISBN-13: 978-0-7407-7385-3
    ISBN-10: 0-7407-7385-2
  1. Ghosts—United States. I. Title.
    BF1472.U6R855 2008
    133.10973—dc22

                                                                2008027928

www.andrewsmcmeel.com
Book design by Holly Camerlinck
Photography by Leslie Rule

ATTENTION: SCHOOLS AND BUSINESSES
Andrews McMeel books are available at quantity discounts with bulk purchase for educational, business, or sales promotional use. For information, please write to: Special Sales Department, Andrews McMeel Publishing, LLC, 1130 Walnut Street, Kansas City, Missouri 64106.

For my friend, Celia Ann Grandon Sadlou

CONTENTS

FOREWORD

BY ANN RULE

I've always felt it must be extremely difficult for ghosts, spirits, the departed, or whatever the proper term is for those who have passed over, to make contact with us in our world. They come to us in dreams, I think, or in that half-asleep state when we are open to things unexplainable.

And they come to us in mirrors.

A broken mirror offers as many images as there are shards of glass, and it is, of course, unlucky. Seven years of bad luck. Why is that? A shattered cup or plate isn't unlucky, but the sight of a mirror in pieces haunts us all, and we don't know why.

Lewis Carroll captured our curiosity about what really lies behind mirrors in *Alice's Adventures in Wonderland* and *Through the Looking-Glass*. Oddly, Lewis Carroll and Alice always frightened me; his books and characters seemed to be somehow schizophrenic. You couldn't count on anything staying the same. The Cheshire Cat appeared and disappeared at will. The queen's croquet mallet turned into a flamingo. The world behind the mirror was confusing and unstable.

When I was a child, I believed that although the immediate image in the glass was identical to the room I was in, there was another house, a different house, if I could only see around the corners and through the walls in the mirror image. And sometimes I still do.

Like my daughter, I am a writer. And we both have vivid imaginations. It seems natural for me to wonder about the other voices and other rooms that are so close, and yet so hidden.

Wouldn't a mirror be an effortless point of entry for a ghost? Surely, gliding through that other world hidden behind the glass would be a path allowing a ghost to both appear and vanish within the blink of an eye. Although I write true crime, I often use the device of an intended victim's terror at the sight of an enemy's reflection approaching from behind.

It's always more frightening than facing an attack head-on.

Or in a movie, perhaps a killer is hiding in a closet or behind a door, and the victim fails to detect that someone else is in the room. Then the camera pans to a dressing table mirror, and a face, or a hand with a knife, appears.

And the audience gasps as one.

I have talked to hundreds of people who knew murder victims, and some of them have been aware of a presence or an image standing close beside them in their mirrors. A ghost come to say good-bye? Or wishful thinking?

When I lived in New York State, I was unfortunate enough to have neighbors who seemed to be either the epitome of evil or the meanest humans I ever met. They complained about everything, ambushed my guests, and reported my dogs as vicious (when they were as docile as bunny rabbits). Any encounter with them was guaranteed to ruin the sunniest day. I did my best to avoid them, and tried to visualize them as inanimate objects such as trees or telephone poles when I found myself within shouting distance. But nothing worked.

Finally, a friend who believed in things both seen and unseen told me what to do. "Buy a mirror," she said. "And place it against the nearest outside wall that faces their house."

After I'd purchased a thrift store mirror and carried it into my living room, I asked, "What good will this do?"

"It won't do any good," she said, "the way you have it now. It's facing out into your room."

"So? That's what mirrors do."

"Not for this purpose. Turn it so it faces the wall. Anything they send to you—negative thoughts, lies, gossip—will go right back to them."

"Isn't that kind of spooky?"

"No. It's only spooky if they choose to send dark thoughts to you. All you've done is lean a mirror against a wall."

Still doubting, I left it there, the tattered brown paper on the back showing. But it worked. Whatever was going on in their house wasn't happening in mine, and I rarely saw them after that.

Probably just a coincidence.

❧

Sometimes, when the light is just right or when there is no light at all, windows become mirrors. I wasn't happy at all back in the '70s when my eldest daughter wanted to move into a place of her own. She was seventeen, just out of high school, and sick of the teasing she endured from her little brothers. Finally, I capitulated after she found a tiny house not that far from where we lived. It was part of the meager estate of an elderly woman who had died a few months earlier.

My daughter worked nights as a waitress and I insisted on picking her up and delivering her safely home after dark. I watched until she was inside and the lights were turned on.

At first, her rented house had seemed welcoming, but within a few weeks a pall seemed to settle over it. The windows let in more shadows than sunlight, and there were cold spots where there was no reason for them to be there. I found some human teeth hidden far back in the bathroom cabinet and shuddered when I saw that the roots were still attached.

Even the food in her refrigerator seemed to spoil far sooner than it normally should have.

She had neighbors who reminded me of the older couple in *Rosemary's Baby*. Their daughter had gone away years before, and they were sitting a kind of vigil until she came home again. Sometimes, I worried that they were trying to adopt *my* daughter.

I was relieved when she moved back home with us after a few months. But there was an afternoon when Leslie and I went back to check the mailbox to see if any bills or letters had arrived after her sister left. It was late in the fall and the sun set early in Seattle, casting shadows. The house was supposed to be empty, but someone—or something—was inside as we pulled up and parked. I caught movement in the front window. Looking back, I know it couldn't have been a reflection from across the street or from a car passing by. It was a face peering out at us. The person wasn't standing or sitting, but seemed to be crouched at the window and his (or her—I couldn't tell which) expression was one of fury.

We never went back again. Maybe it was a squatter, a homeless person who had taken the opportunity to move into a vacant house. I don't know. It didn't seem human to me, and I figured I'd seen a ghost. Later, I mentioned what I'd seen to Leslie and she said she'd seen it, too. Frankly, it was too menacing to discuss. And it would be years before Leslie and I really talked about what each of us had seen in the window of that shabby little house.

Now, I do my writing in a cottage next door to the house where I live. The elderly couple who lived here for more than fifty years are both dead, but we were good friends and neighbors for a dozen years. Not too long after the old man died, I often smelled the fragrance of his pipe, but it didn't scare me. If he was around, his was a beneficent presence. Her roses bloom in my garden, and I remember her Valentine's Day lunches for the neighbor ladies.

I miss them, but I don't see their faces in the mirrors they left behind. If they come back to visit occasionally, it's okay with me. They loved their years here on Puget Sound.

INTRODUCTION

In a child's mind, the mirror is a separate realm, filled with mimickers set on fooling us. Each person in our world is assigned a twin who dresses as we do and dutifully copies our every move when we gaze at them through the glass.

It is a fanciful and flawed scenario that nearly every child embraces at least once. Children don't question it until they are too old to play the game. In the meantime, children everywhere attempt to trick their reflection into making a mistake.

If they can just turn around fast enough, perhaps they can catch their reflection off guard. Perhaps they can sneak a peek at their mirror twin doing something entirely different.

As adults, we realize that the mirror is simply a sheet of glass, coated on the back with silvering to create a reflective surface. We know that the mirror is *not* a window to another world.

Or is it?

Perhaps we adults are not as smart as we think we are. Perhaps the mirror *is* an opening to another universe. Perhaps the perfectly synchronized backward copy of our world *is* actually another place.

Separate world or special effect?

We cannot say for certain that reflection is either. For there is no way to actually visit the mirror world. We can only peer in. If we try to force our way through, we shatter the doorway, leaving reflective shards that cut our feet and offer no new clues.

We cannot enter the mirror. Yet there are others who can. They have been seen there by sober and sane witnesses as far back as history can reach. The Others, some say, can also *exit* the mirror, stepping into our domain to mingle with us.

Maybe the ghost in the mirror isn't really *in* the mirror—no more than we are actually in the mirror. Like us, the ghost only appears to be there, but for some inexplicable reason can be more easily witnessed in reflective mode.

I do not have the answer, only many more questions.

I *do* know that when it comes to sightings of apparitions, we see countless cases of ghosts in mirrors. It is these cases that have led some to theorize that the mirror is a portal to another plain. Spirits from the Other Side visit without knocking, popping up behind us as we brush our teeth or comb our hair, startling us as we glance into the mirror and see them there behind us.

Does one ghost in the mirror lead others over the threshold? Does it start with a single ghost entering our plain through a sheet of reflective glass?

If it does not in life, it *will* in this book.

As we explore the spirits from the Other Side and their interactions with our world, a mirror ghost will lead each chapter. The elusive spirit that haunts the mirror will beckon the others to follow.

Whether they are bumping about our attics, hitchhiking on a moonlit road, or fraternizing with our reflections, ghosts tantalize us with their secrets.

The following cases not only reflect upon the mysterious ways of ghosts, they also shed light upon the lives of the humans they once were. Whether you smile, cry, or shiver as their stories unfold, I hope, at the very least, you will be entertained.

GHOST
IN THE
MIRROR

GHOSTS AND CHILDREN

Though about one in three people admit they have seen a ghost, the number of sightings could actually be much higher. In some instances, apparitions are so lifelike that they are mistaken for live people, and in millions of other cases the witnesses simply don't *remember* their spirit encounters.

Few people remember the details of early childhood, and as they age, they forget the ghosts they have met.

Visits from the spirits of loving grandparents are near the top of the list when it comes to encounters with ghosts. Many parents have told me how their babies and toddlers seem to be talking to a grandparent who died before the child was born, giggling and calling them by the special nickname the child should not know.

It makes perfect sense. Of course the grandparent would want to visit, and, naturally, the child would be able to see them. For the innocents among us are privy to things that most of us cannot sense.

Animals and kids are wide open to spirit encounters, though the older the child, the less likely they are to see a ghost. Kids lose the ability to see, partly because they are taught by adults "not to make up stories."

In the following case, two young girls meet in an unlikely place. One of them told me her story.

STRANGER IN THE SHOWER

It was the first day of school and Kya Dunagan was running late. As her mother urged her to hurry, she stepped into the bathroom of their south Seattle apartment, flicked on the light, and reached for her hairbrush. The seven-year-old looked into the mirror, pulled the brush through her long blond hair, and froze.

There, reflected in the glass, was an unfamiliar girl.

"She was in the shower behind me," Kya told me.

The strange girl's lips were curved into a friendly smile. She wore a nightgown and her auburn hair curled about her pretty face. Instinctively, Kya turned around to look at the shower.

No one was there.

Kya glanced back at the mirror. The girl was still there, captured in the reflection and smiling expectantly. In a moment of confused silence, Kya could only stand there, her fingers curled around the handle of the hairbrush, her arm paused in midair.

Then the girl spoke. It was a single word, sweet, yet piercing. "Hi."

Kya dropped the brush and ran.

Her mom was waiting for her at the front door and Kya told her that she had seen a girl in the mirror. Jennifer Dunagan was running late, trying to juggle coats and keys and money for school lunches. Though she appreciated her daughter's imagination, she was not in the mood to indulge her.

"She didn't believe me," said Kya.

Three years later, ten-year-old Kya explained to me that when the girl appeared she had had an imaginary friend, so she was not surprised her mother was skeptical. "My imaginary friend's name was Olla, and she looked a little like the girl in the mirror, but Olla's hair was long and dark."

Kya Dunagan will never forget the stranger she met in her family's Seattle apartment. (Leslie Rule)

With all of the wisdom of a fifth grader, Kya told me that she definitely knows the difference between an imaginary being and an apparition in the mirror. The mirror girl was real, she insisted, and she remembers her with detailed clarity.

Jennifer no longer doubts her daughter. Kya, like all of the females in her family, is psychic. "She can sense something wrong when we pass a bad person on the street," said Jennifer, describing how Kya's thin shoulders sometimes shudder when they encounter a seemingly benign stranger.

The Dunagans have moved from the apartment complex where the mirror girl appeared. And after that one exciting morning, the apparition was not seen again.

In retrospect, Jennifer remembers other odd things that occurred in the apartment. "The TV turned itself on and off," she said. "I still have the TV and it doesn't do that anymore." That makes Jennifer wonder if the apartment is haunted.

I went by the apartment complex, spoke with the managers, and searched newspaper archives but have yet to find an account of a girl who died near the spot.

The hillside apartments are fairly new. A century ago a few cabins were sprinkled upon the sloping terrain, homesteaded by pioneers without permits, and demolished before most of us were born. The memory of the long-gone homes is buried beneath asphalt, concrete, and four-story buildings. A little girl who once lived, and perhaps *died* there, may be the only one who remembers.

Paranormal researchers have noted that spirit activity escalates on anniversaries and holidays. Perhaps the mirror girl was enticed by the excitement of the first day of school. It's possible she was one of the many children of early Seattle, stricken with a deadly disease—maybe just before school began.

When you look at Kya's family history, it is not surprising that she met a ghost. It seems that such encounters run in the family. Jennifer was just three years old and living in Wenatchee, Washington, when she began talking to her parents about Grandma.

"I don't remember it, but my parents said I drove them crazy talking about her all the time." Jennifer's own grandmothers had little contact with the family and her parents thought it was only the little girl's wishful thinking and overactive imagination.

Then one day the toddler became particularly insistent. "Let's go to Grandma's house," Jennifer cried.

Her parents were exasperated, but in a moment of indulgence they got into the car and followed her directions as she shouted from the backseat, "Turn here. Go down the next block. Ok, now turn here."

Eventually they ended up in an orchard.

Jennifer's mom, Jacki Cote, felt a prickle at the back of her neck when she saw the rows of gnarled apple trees. She had been there before. Though the land was now vacant, she had visited a home there years ago. She had been just a child herself when her family was friendly with an elderly woman who lived there.

The sweet little old lady had welcomed them warmly into her cozy home by the apple orchard. *Could she be the grandma Jennifer talked about?* Jacki wondered.

Oddly, after the trip to the orchard, little Jennifer never again mentioned Grandma. Is it possible that the spirit of the old woman had gotten lost? Had she visited a familiar family, discovered that only the child could see her, and hitched a ride home, prodding Jennifer to give directions? If so, maybe when she saw that her house was long gone, she realized that time had passed and she was finally able to move on.

❧

I still wonder about the story my baby brother told us many years ago when we lived in a beach house in Des Moines, Washington. I can still see two-year-old Mike, with his wild red curls, a sprinkling of freckles across his upturned nose, and his brown eyes startlingly solemn as he pointed at the hole in the brick wall of the basement bedroom I shared with my sister. A wood-burning stove had once been affixed there, and the stovepipe vented through the hole. The stove was long gone, but the hole was still there, cold and unblinking like an empty eye socket staring vacuously into the room. For some reason that I don't recall, the decorative plate that normally covered the hole had been absent for a number of months.

I was already spooked by the dark hole before Mike opened up his little baby mouth and said, "A monkey went into the hole."

When my siblings and I questioned him, the details emerged. He had seen a "monkey" cross the room, climb the brick wall, and disappear into the hole.

Maybe it would not have chilled us as much if Mike had not been so serious about it. His usual silly demeanor disappeared and he stuck to his story.

Was Mike making up a story? Or was he recounting a dream? My parents made no secret that the house was haunted as readers of my book *Coast to Coast Ghosts: True Stories of Hauntings Across America* may recall.

Before we moved in, my parents had rented the house to a family who lost a baby. The child, who was about a year old, had died of an illness while sleeping in the room directly above the basement bedroom where Mike had seen the monkey. Had my little brother seen the ghost of the baby creeping across the floor?

Today Mike has no memory of the incident, though he loves to hear me tell the story. Mike is not alone. Most people cannot remember their early childhood—let alone any ghosts they may have met when they were toddlers. I clearly remember my life at age three, my opinions about the world, and things I saw that I still can't explain.

I was not quite three when I witnessed something that seemed normal at the time, yet confuses me now. For years I thought it must have been a dream. But the more I research the paranormal, the more I wonder about what I saw. We lived in Bellevue, Washington, in a ranch-style home my grandfather built for us. The area, rich with pine and fir trees, was called Robinswood, and at the time, was filled with more forest than houses.

It was the middle of the night and I got up and wandered into the kitchen. My parents were smokers back then, and owned an ashtray with a ceramic Native American head attached. The figure, which looked like a chief in full-feathered headdress, "gazed" stoically at the ashtray on the dining room table. On this particular night, I saw a cowboy on the kitchen counter, though only his head and right arm were visible. He and the chief were engaged in battle, bullets flying back and forth between them. When the chief was hit, the ashtray fell to the floor, shattering into pieces.

The next morning I found my mother in the kitchen, sweeping the broken pieces into the dustpan. "The cowboy shot him," I told her.

"The cat broke it," she replied.

I tried to explain what I had seen but she was stubborn and insisted that the cat had jumped on the table during the night and knocked the ashtray off.

Had I been sleepwalking? Perhaps I had knocked the ashtray down myself while dreaming. When it broke, I awoke and saw the pieces. I was known to sleepwalk during that time, and remember waking up in odd places.

Or had I somehow witnessed a snippet of the past? Had there been a violent confrontation on that spot when it was still the Wild West?

When it comes to ghost encounters, many believe a thin veil separates the dream world from the Other Side. And indeed, children who see strange things in the night are usually consoled by an adult who insists, "It was just a dream."

Children can suffer from night terrors, a common sleep disturbance that is marked by a terrified scream. This sudden arousal from slow-wave sleep normally occurs early in the night and though the child seems to be awake, they will likely not recall the experience. (Parents suspecting this problem should consult a pediatrician.) Not all nighttime frights, however, can be dismissed as such.

In the following case a young girl saw something that still spooks her, though decades have passed. Despite what the adults said, she is sure she was *not* dreaming.

EYE TO EYE

When Dhebi Siconolfi was a child she did not have to travel far to visit her best friend. Their families shared a duplex in Southbridge, Massachusetts. Dhebi's family lived on the floor above Nona's family, and it was not unusual for the girls to spend the night with each other. Yet one night was so unusual that Dhebi cannot forget it, despite the fact that four decades have passed.

After an evening of watching television, giggling, and snacking on popcorn, the eight-year-olds fell asleep side by side in Nona's bed.

"Sometime during the night I woke up," said Dhebi. A figure darted across the room, deliberately moving toward her. The lights were out, and Dhebi could not see who it was. "I wasn't alarmed," she said. "I figured it was Wayne, Nona's big brother."

He was several years older than the girls and liked to tease them and play pranks. So Dhebi was not worried when she saw someone stoop over and scoot beneath the bed.

I wonder what he is up to, she thought. She ignored him and rolled over to lie face down on the bed. Her eyes were wide open but she should not have been able to see a single thing. Yet, suddenly, she could see right *through* the mattress and was horrified to see a pair of eyes staring back at her. The disembodied eyes were not cloaked in darkness, but as clear and vivid as if she were viewing them in daylight.

When Dhebi screamed, her shrieks roused the household. As Nona sat up in bed beside her, the lights in the room came on and Nona's parents were huddled in the doorway, peering in at them.

"There's someone under the bed!" Dhebi cried.

"It was just a nightmare," they told her. Nona's father dutifully peeked beneath the bed and reassured her, "There's no one there."

"I *saw* it!" Dhebi protested. "I saw eyes!" She tried to tell them about what she had witnessed. She knew it sounded impossible yet she had seen it. The eyes were topped by brows and spaced like a normal pair of eyes. She had also seen the bridge of the nose in between, but the rest of the face was invisible.

Nona's mom shook her head. "We told you girls not to watch that scary movie," she scolded. "See what happens? You had a nightmare."

"I was awake and it was real," Dhebi protested as the adults patiently tucked them back in bed.

Today, Dhebi is the mother of three grown children and she is still adamant that she was awake and alert when a phantom being crept across the room and slid beneath her bed. She remembers the eyes, unblinking as they stared back at her, burning through the mattress.

The vision was not from a nightmare induced by the scary movie, though she remembers that the flick *did* frighten them. "It was *The House of Wax*, an old horror flick with Vincent Price. We weren't supposed to watch it, but we left the bedroom door open so we could see across the hall into the living room where the adults had the TV on," Dhebi remembered.

The details of the movie have faded, but the eyes have seared a permanent place in her memory.

❧

When it comes to ghost sightings, many people report seeing partial apparitions. The following case is another example.

EDWARD'S PUNISHMENT

Over half a century has passed since Louise Inman Strother witnessed something peculiar that both frightened and pleased her. The Oakdale, Louisiana, mother of two has always lived in the South. She grew up in Mermentau, Louisiana, near her cousin Edward and her aunt Carrie.

"My older cousin almost died when he was born because he was so tiny," Louise told me. "I remember the adults saying that he was so little that he could fit on a dinner plate. They worried about him so much that they ended up spoiling him."

The sickly infant grew into a strong, husky boy who was used to getting his way. And when he *didn't*, he bullied his widowed mother until she gave in.

While her cousin had grown healthy, Louise's aunt had developed health problems and Louise felt sorry for her. "My aunt was precious," she emphasized. "She didn't deserve to be treated like that."

By the time Louise was eight years old, her cousin towered over her. One day when she visited her aunt, she heard her cousin speaking harshly to his mother. "He cussed at her, and I hated it," she said. "He was so ugly to her."

But there was nothing she could do but stand by helplessly and watch as Edward mouthed off. Suddenly, as he was spewing obscenities, Louise heard a loud smack. Her cousin grabbed the side of his face and staggered backward.

The boy's mother raised her eyebrows. "What's the matter?" she asked him.

"Someone slapped me!" cried the stunned boy.

His mother shook her finger at him and said, "That was your dead daddy!"

"It scared me," Louise told me. "But I was so happy it happened."

Recently she asked her cousin if he remembered the ghostly slap.

"Sure," he replied. "How could I forget?"

In fact, Edward told her that it was not the last time it happened. Shortly after the first incident, he was in his room when he saw a disembodied hand fly through the air and smack him.

"I wish I could say that it straightened him out," said Louise. "But it didn't."

Today her cousin is over seventy and suffers from the same ailments that plagued his mother. Louise doesn't know if he feels any guilt over his spoiled behavior.

She often finds herself wondering who the punishing hand belonged to. Was it her deceased uncle's hand, as her aunt said, or was it the hand of an unknown spirit attached to the property? The mystery, she said, sparked a lifelong fascination with ghosts.

Maybe it is not kind of me, but I can't help the smile of satisfaction when I picture the hand smacking the rude boy. The following cases, however, cause me to quickly lose that smile. They reverberate with the kind of creepiness that sparks nightmares.

RESTLESS NIGHTS

Traci Bartolone never felt safe when she went to sleep in her bed in her childhood home in Hammonton, New Jersey. "When I was about nine years old, I used to wake to someone touching my feet under the covers."

She knew, of course, that she was alone in the bed and hoped the sensation was just the blankets tangled about her feet. Still, it scared her, and whenever she felt the fingers on her feet, she called to her older sister, Michelle, who snoozed in the bed next to hers.

"I could never get her to wake up," Traci told me, as she described how she would scrunch up in the bed with her knees to her chest, wishing the light from her nightlight burned brighter.

"One night I felt something pull real hard on my big toe," she told me. "I was tired of being scared. I got mad." Traci lifted the covers and peered down at her feet "That's when I saw a hand quickly retreating to wherever it had come from."

Traci shrieked for her sister, but Michelle would not wake up.

The image of the withdrawing hand has stayed with her and she is positive it was not a dream. "I saw a whole hand and wrist," she said. "It was masculine, solid, and pale. I actually saw it snap back when it let go of my toe and quickly went straight down, almost as if it was scared that I saw it."

Michelle also experienced odd things in the room. The television and radio would constantly turn themselves on, but this was nowhere near as frightening as her sister's episodes.

Today Traci is a grown woman and the mother of a toddler. Yet she cannot shake the image of the phantom hand. "I still sleep with the lights on," she admitted.

Jason Perrone, Traci's fiancé, does not provide much reassurance.

For he, too, is haunted by a childhood specter, and he cannot sleep with the bedroom door open.

Lights on and door firmly shut! That is the rule in their household and it must be adhered to if anyone is to get any rest. Jason is a twenty-five-year-old frozen food clerk at an upscale grocery store near his home in Medford, New Jersey. While handling frozen food all day may give him the chills, nothing makes him shiver like the memory of a nighttime visitor. The haunting began when he was a small boy while he lived in an apartment complex in Edgewood Park, New Jersey.

"The first time I saw her I was six years old," he told me. He shared a room with his older brother, Tom, who had a much later bedtime. Their mother tucked Jason into bed early and then left his bedroom door ajar so he would have light from the hallway.

As the little boy lay in bed, he was startled to see an elderly woman walk past the open door. When the shriveled being ambled by, he saw that she had curly white hair that fell past her shoulders. She wore a silky, white nightgown and carried a large wicker basket clutched to her chest. "She walked past my door a couple of times and then she looked in at me," Jason said.

Her eyes frightened him the most. The white orbs contained no pupils, yet they seemed to bore into him. "It was as if she stared into my soul," he said.

Jason was immobilized by fear, unable to dive beneath the covers or call out. Later, he tried to tell his mother about what he had seen. "She thought I was making it up," he said.

Over the years, the spirit appeared frequently, always following the same pattern and always carrying the basket. No one else in the family ever saw the old woman, though he sometimes tried to wake his brother when she appeared.

"I wanted someone else to see her so that they would believe me,"

Jason said. "But I could never wake up my brother. He was always in a deep sleep, almost like a trance."

The Perrone family moved twice, and Jason was dismayed to find that he could not escape his night visitor. For the old woman moved with them and continued to appear outside of the frightened boy's bedroom.

Jason continued to tell his family that the entity was real, and eventually his mother began to entertain the idea that he was actually witnessing something, but she did not grasp the full horror of the encounter.

"She said it was my great aunt Bess looking out for me," he told me, still sounding somewhat bitter as he explained that the apparition did resemble his deceased aunt. He did not know who the being was, but he did not believe she had his best interests in mind.

She was a creepy phantom, a nightmare image that he could not shake. He never got over his fear and wished his brothers would remember to keep the bedroom door shut. But inevitably, someone would leave the door ajar and he would find himself terror struck with the empty eyes fixed upon him.

"The last time I saw her, I was fourteen," Jason said. He believes that as he grew older he lost his ability to see those who lurk on the Other Side.

I was intrigued by Jason's and Traci's encounters. Each had experienced something odd that was unlike anything I have previously researched.

I have heard hundreds of firsthand accounts of spirit sightings and choose only the most compelling and believable cases for my books. I questioned both Jason and Traci carefully. Neither wavered from the details of their accounts and both came across as sincere.

I sometimes suspect that stories too scary or too detailed are made up and abandon the idea of including them in a book. Despite the extreme "creep factor" of the couple's experiences, I believe them.

I researched the backgrounds of their childhood homes where the encounters occurred in an effort to make sense of cases so spooky that they gave *me* nightmares.

In Jason's case, the apparition's eyes puzzled me. No one before him had ever described such eyes to me.

Usually the description of a ghost matches the appearance of the live human being it represents—though it sometimes is missing feet, or manifests as colorless or pale. This made me wonder if Jason had seen the ghost of a blind woman.

Could unseeing eyes appear as the blank, white orbs that Jason described?

Some quick research verified that blind eyes can indeed appear as white orbs. The condition can occur as a result of a severe infection of the cornea, an accident, or, in rarer instances, as an inherited defect.

What about the basket?

Although Jason was unable to see the contents, he assumed it was a laundry basket. He described it as wicker, with the circumference larger at the top.

More research revealed that basket weaving has long been a common trade among the sight impaired in the general area. For instance, in the neighboring state, the New York School for the Blind in Batavia opened in 1868 and is dedicated to teaching students skills so they can become independent. Basket weaving was among some of the early trades taught there.

The ghost of an elderly blind woman may have been wandering the grounds for some time before Jason saw her—quite possibly for centuries. He may have been the first person to see her and as a result she felt a connection with him and followed him to his new residences.

Though the apparition's eyes appeared blind, she most likely could see as well as any other ghost—though a ghost's way of seeing is beyond our understanding.

Sometimes ghosts are seen with props, such as the basket in the old woman's arms. These props, somewhat like the clothing apparitions wear, become part of the manifestation. If a basket was ever present in the woman's arms in life, it is not surprising it should materialize with her in death.

Who was the frightening entity who tormented Traci Bartolone?

The land in Hammonton was surrounded by marshes and woods, with the Wharton State Forest beyond. Traci's grandfather had had a house on the land. And Traci's father had later cleared a spot in the woods to build their home.

"My neighbors once told me that their children had found arrowheads in the woods behind our house," said Traci. "That was in the 1950s and 1960s."

My research shows that the Lenni-Lenape tribe had roamed the area long before the first Europeans settled there. They had generously welcomed pioneers and showed them how to build temporary housing and how to farm the land.

It was a fatal mistake. While the tribe showed the newcomers how to live, the pioneers showed them how to *die*. The Lenni-Lenape had no natural immunities and more than half of their population succumbed to diseases such as smallpox and measles.

"My family is part Sioux and we're from the Rosebud tribe," said Traci, explaining that she wondered if the spirit of a Native American who died on the land was drawn to her long black hair and chiseled cheekbones, perhaps mistaking her for someone else.

❧

When it comes to childhood encounters with ghosts, many children have trouble finding an adult to believe them. The overwhelming skepticism of the grown-ups leaves the kids doubting themselves.

Adults are very good at explaining away things they'd rather not think about. But what if an entire group of children witnessed the same thing as in the following story?

GRANDMA'S HOUSE

When most people remember time spent at grandma's house, their memories are pleasant. Some folks think of fresh-baked cookies and others smile as they reminisce about grandma's prize-winning tomatoes or the wonderful stories she told. And almost everyone remembers feeling safe.

When Marilyn Covarrubias thinks of her grandma's house, however, she remembers the scariest moment of her life.

Marilyn was barely school age in the 1950s when she and an assortment of siblings and cousins were often dropped off for long stays with her grandparents in their rented home in Los Angeles, California. "It was an old house," she told me. "And it was right across the street from Hazard Park." The twenty-five-acre park, with rolling green hills and countless trees to climb, was named for Henry Thomas Hazard one of Los Angeles' first mayors. The park was enticing to the children, who often sneaked over there to play when the adults left them on their own.

"We were left alone a lot," she confided. It was a little spooky, considering that the house made more than its share of odd noises expected of an aging structure. "We heard a woman and a baby crying," she said, shivering at the thought of the phantom sobs emanating from an empty room.

"One day my grandma pulled a piece of cardboard off of a hole in the wall and found old clothes inside the wall," said Marilyn. "She pulled out a woman's clothes and baby clothes."

The family wondered if the clothing had been hidden there for a sinister reason. Did it have something to do with the ghostly cries?

Perhaps it was simply insulation. In bygone days, used clothing was sometimes recycled as insulation. The house, Marilyn remembers, was made of heavy wood, with plank floors, like homes built in the nineteenth century, and it had probably seen many families come and go.

Yet at least one of those families left something more than clothing behind. There was definitely something odd about the place, and Marilyn's family suspected the house was haunted.

The mysterious crying was not the only sign that something unknown lurked at grandma's house. Marilyn's mother was the first to actually see something strange there. She was napping on the living room couch when she awoke to find a woman and a dog in the process of crossing the room. "My mother told me that the dog stopped and licked her hand," said Marilyn. As the ghostly woman walked by, the canine followed and then, suddenly, they both vanished.

"I never saw the ghosts of the woman and the dog," Marilyn said. "But I saw something else."

The third-floor attic was a favorite place for the gang of kids to play. "My grandparents kept two big beds up there, and they pushed them together in the middle of the room." Marilyn and the other children loved to jump on the beds and race around the attic.

One evening, when Marilyn was six years old, the kids again found themselves alone. "It was Grandma's bingo night," explained

Marilyn. "There were six of us playing in the attic." The bunch ranged in age from her little sister Karen who was just a year old to her cousin Reuben who was eight. Donny, Reuben, Marian, Marilyn, Tony, and Karen were all happily playing when they heard the familiar sound of heavy footsteps pounding up the stairs.

"My grandpa was a big man with size fourteen shoes," said Marilyn. "He always made a lot of noise when he came up those stairs."

Since the children were up past their bedtime, they quickly dove into the beds and pulled the covers up to their chins as they listened to their grandpa's approaching steps. "We were all giggling and trying to pretend we were asleep."

But when the door flew open, it was not Grandpa.

A stranger stood in the doorway. The man looked as if he had been caught in a downpour. "He was so wet that his hair was matted to his forehead," said Marilyn. He wore a plaid shirt like a lumberjack, and his eyes were bloodshot. "They were so bloodshot that they were completely red," she stressed.

As he stood there, the stranger made a sound that is hard for Marilyn to describe, yet impossible for her to forget. "It was as if he were laughing and crying at the same time," she explained.

The children were dumbstruck by the image of the wild man with the maniacal cry. They watched in horror as he suddenly bolted toward them. When he reached the beds, he did not stop: He ran right *through* the beds. "We could feel him," said Marilyn, describing the sensation as a rush of cold wind.

The man dove for the window and as he broke through the glass, they heard it shattering around them. And then, the only sound was the steady patter of rain.

Was the man outside, broken and dead on the ground, far below the attic window?

The kids were too scared to get out of bed and look. They huddled beneath the blankets, waiting for what seemed like hours.

"Then we heard footsteps on the stairs again," said Marilyn.

The children were petrified and barely able to breathe as heavy feet thundered up the stairs toward them. Again, the door flew open. This time it was Grandpa. "We jumped out of bed and ran to him. We were all crying."

Their grandfather shook his head as they told their wild story. "It was just your imagination," he consoled them and led them to the window. "See," he said patiently. "The glass isn't broken. And it's not raining outside."

He was right. The window was intact and the night was dry.

Grandpa must be right, six-year-old Marilyn decided. There was no man. They had imagined the whole thing.

Even decades later, Marilyn could not forget the crazed man who dove through the attic window. She was reminiscing with her cousin Tony at a family gathering when he said something about the ghost in the attic.

She gasped. "I thought I imagined that!"

"Oh, no!" he assured her. "It really happened."

Tony recalled the scene exactly as she did, and told her that he and Reuben had discussed it many times over the years.

What happened at that house? Did a man kill himself by leaping through the attic window? If so, what made him do it? Did something awful happen to him? Or did he do something bad to someone else to drive him to suicide out of guilt?

Despite my research, I have yet to determine if a man did indeed leap through a window in Marilyn's grandparents' house. I am still searching for answers.

❧

Though most children wish that an adult would believe their stories of spirit encounters, for some it makes no difference. In the following case, the adults in a young boy's life were nearly as frightening as the ghosts.

PEEPING TOM

The following is an excerpt of a letter sent to me by Mark Miner in the spring of 2007. He is not quite forty and currently resides in Oregon. He has lived in many places throughout his life, but Wichita, Kansas, may be the most memorable for that is where he saw his very first ghost.

My research verified that the neighbor with the unusual last name existed and did indeed die the year Mark was eight years old. I have changed the neighbor's name, to protect the privacy of any surviving relatives.

I was born into a poor and angry family. There were seven of us kids, and our parents constantly fought. My siblings and I had good times together, but not many with our parents. We also tended to move around a lot.

My mother was interested in the paranormal, but we kids were not aware of this until we were grown.

The story begins when I was nine years old. We had been living in Wichita, Kansas, for three months. I hated living there. I was constantly picked on at school. And then I'd come home to an abusive father and a mother who ignored us.

One day my mother was in a really bad mood. I could not deal with the thought of a drama-filled evening. I thought that if I picked flowers for her that her mood would brighten.

Mr. Langley, an older man who lived across the street, had recently died. He always gave me the spooks when he talked to my parents in our front yard. My parents were not bothered by him until the night my father caught Mr. Langley peering in the window of the bedroom I shared with my three sisters.

My father flipped and chased Mr. Langley off of our property. It was not an option for us to call the police. We were always taught to take care of our own problems.

A month later, Mr. Langley died of cancer. No one realized how bad off he was for he never showed any signs of being sick.

His house sat empty as his grass grew tall.

On the day I decided to pick flowers for my mother, I noticed that the prettiest ones bloomed in Mr. Langley's yard. I reasoned that the old man was dead and couldn't possibly hurt me now.

I ran as fast as I could across the street, so that my mother wouldn't notice. I squatted down in the yard, hidden from view by the tall grass. I was totally engrossed in picking flowers when I heard someone say, "Hello."

I looked up and there was Mr. Langley, standing not three feet from me. He looked so real. I was stunned and did not know how to process what I was seeing. After what seemed like an eternity, I jumped up and raced home, dropping the flowers as I went.

I ran through the back door to see my mother sitting at the kitchen table. When she asked me what was wrong, I did not hesitate. I told her I had seen Mr. Langley's ghost.

She looked at me sternly and slapped me. She asked me if I knew what I had done wrong. I answered that I had gone onto Mr. Langley's property. But that was not the answer she was looking for.

My mother explained that I was supposed to stay and ask Mr. Langley if he needed anything from me. She said that it was my responsibility as a seer of spirits.

I was confused. She told me to not say anything to anybody about the encounter. I promised that I wouldn't.

A few nights later, I was having trouble sleeping and realized that someone unknown was in the room. My sisters were asleep. I heard what sounded like someone rustling past the window inside the room. I fixed my eyes there, but saw nothing. So I closed my eyes tight and wished it away. Then I felt a light kiss on my right cheek. I turned to look and saw no one.

I spent tormented hours with the sound of whispering around me. Many voices were speaking and I could not understand any of them because they all spoke at once.

I got up and ran into the living room where my brother slept on the couch. I started crying and couldn't stop until my mother got up and told me to sleep with her. I felt safe in my parents' bed. My mother went to get a glass of water and I glanced at the window. Mr. Langley was there, staring through the glass at me.

I never mentioned that night to anyone until I became an adult. Finally I shared the experience with one of my sisters. She laughed and said that I was "just a highly imaginative child."

While many of the cases recounted here are creepy and frightening, not all spirit visits fill witnesses with dread. Some are uplifting, such as the following. Though it occurred decades ago, it left a sweet persistent memory.

BLISSFUL BOND

When Cecelia Meurling was a little girl, she loved to visit her grandparents' farm on Gueme's Island. The small, secluded island is lesser known than the other popular tourist destination San Juan Islands that are scattered across Puget Sound like irregular puddles of pancake batter on the grill. Gueme's Island is just north across the channel from Anacortes, Washington, and was first settled by Cecelia's great-grandfather.

"My grandparents lived in a one-story house, painted white. It sat back some distance from the road and it was about a half mile up the hill from the ferry," said Cecelia, who today is the mother of a grown son. The Burien, Washington, cat shelter volunteer can close her eyes and still see Dolly and Bonny, her grandfather's sturdy white plow horses. "He had chickens, too, and it was my job to watch for hawks and tell him right away when I saw one."

The picturesque farm, surrounded by pastures and cornfields, had been in the family for generations. In fact, Cecelia's mother had been born in the house. Dozens of cousins and aunts and uncles had also grown up on the island. Her grandparents, Bob and Mary Merchant, knew everyone who lived there.

"I called my grandmother Sela. She was short and plump with curly, dark hair. She loved her flower garden, and when I stayed there, we would get up early, with the chickens! And with our pajamas still on, we'd go out to see how her 'girls' were doing," she said, describing how they would admire the daffodils, roses, and pansies as the sun peeked over the horizon.

Cecelia remembers the swing on the old crabapple tree, and how her grandmother took time from cooking to push her on it. "She would stir a pot, and run out to give me a push, and then run back in and stir some more."

"We were very close," said Cecelia. "We could talk about anything."

Yet there was a time when one topic was off-limits. Cecelia was four years old when she found herself unwilling to speak to anyone about someone very special to her.

One bright spring day, Cecelia told her grandmother that she was going out to play. She stepped outside into the fresh, salty air, and as she skipped toward the fields, she was met by a girl.

"She was not familiar to me," Cecelia said. "Yet it was like she was waiting for me."

The little girls looked into each other's smiling eyes and clasped hands. It was an instant, blissful bond. "I was so happy to see her and she was just as happy to see me. We ran into the field, holding hands, and giggling."

The child was about Cecelia's size, and clad in a pair of blue overalls. Her blond curls bounced, shining in the sunshine as they frolicked. "We never talked," said Cecelia. "We never said a word."

The girls headed toward the barn, and were playing behind it when Cecelia heard her grandmother calling. Grandma Sela's voice was strained with worry.

Cecelia knew that her grandmother liked to keep an eye on her, so she let go of her little friend's hand and stepped out from behind the barn. "I waved to my grandmother to let her know where I was," she said.

She turned back to her friend. The girl with the curly hair was gone.

When Grandma Sela approached to see what her grandchild was up to, Cecelia excitedly told her that she had been playing with her new friend.

Her grandmother glanced around. "I would like to know who you are talking about," she said.

Cecelia grabbed Grandma Sela's hand and pulled her along, saying, "Come and meet her!"

She knew her friend could not have gone far.

But the child had vanished as suddenly as she had appeared.

They gazed about, their eyes searching the pastures and fields stretched out before them. The corn hadn't started to grow again and there wasn't anywhere to hide. So, *where* was she?

"I want to play with her," Cecelia insisted.

"I wish I knew who you were talking about," said Grandma Sela and shook her head. "I can't imagine who she could be."

The nearest neighbors lived far down the road. Grandma Sela knew everyone on the island and had never seen a child like the one Cecelia described.

Yet at age four, Cecelia could not grasp the enormity of the mystery. She knew only that her friend had brought her joy and she could not wait to see her again. She searched Grandma's barn and yard, peeking behind the apple trees, and circling the house, desperately hoping that the giggling girl would pop out from a hiding place. "I never saw her again," Cecelia said sadly. "I was overwhelmingly disappointed that I could not find her."

Later, when she overheard her grandmother telling her mother about the mystery girl, Cecelia felt an odd stirring in her belly. Her grandmother made it sound as if something was wrong.

"To me it had been the most natural thing in the world," Cecelia confided. "But my grandmother made such a big issue of it, I decided not to talk about it anymore." She still missed her friend, but she kept it to herself.

Years later, when her grandmother mentioned the puzzling visit from the little girl, Cecelia told her that she still remembered it.

Grandma Sela's eyes narrowed as she pondered the possibilities.

"I don't know who she could have been," she said. "Unless she was an angel."

It was then that Cecelia began to wonder. Perhaps the little girl had not been of this world. It was hard to imagine. Her hand had been warm and solid when she held it in her own.

Where had the girl come from? How could she have appeared so quickly and then disappear again? Why didn't they see her running away across the fields?

If she was a spirit child, perhaps she was a relative. Cecelia's great-grandmother had given birth to seventeen children on the island and not all had survived childhood.

It seems that whoever she was, the gleeful child was indeed from another place. She had not arrived on the island by ferryboat, as Cecelia had, but had journeyed there from an unknown world in a mysterious fashion. Angel or ghost, Cecelia will never forget her.

"The little girl brought me such a feeling of pure joy and bliss," said Cecelia. "I've never felt that happy since. I wonder if I will ever see her again."

The Apparition Room

When Dr. Raymond Moody published his blockbuster book *Life After Life* in 1975, it reassured millions of readers who were grieving for loved ones. His credible and carefully researched case studies of those who momentarily died and came back to life both intrigued and bolstered us.

He coined the term "near-death experience," and the image of a tunnel leading to a bright light in the hereafter seeped so deeply into the American consciousness that most folks don't remember that it was Dr. Moody who brought it to the forefront. Yet people felt peace with a renewed faith that family and friends who die first wait for the ones who come after and lovingly greet them at the end of the tunnel.

Since then Dr. Moody has continued his research and interviewed many who have had spirit encounters. It did not escape him that, "A surprising number of spontaneous apparitions of the deceased are seen in mirrors or other reflective surfaces," as he wrote in his book *Reunions: Visionary Encounters with Departed Loved Ones.*

He cited the case of Abraham Lincoln, who saw his own ghost in the mirror in 1860 on the night he was elected president. Lincoln was resting on his couch when he glanced at the mirror and saw a double image of himself. One was his expected reflection, while the other beside it was "pale and ghostly."

When Lincon's wife was told of the sighting, she correctly predicted it meant that he would be elected to two terms and die in office.

It occurred to Dr. Moody that spirit encounters could be "facilitated" in a controlled setting, using the mirror as a venue. He created his own psychomanteum, which he sometimes called the "Apparition Room."

The dark room was equipped with a comfortable chair, tilted so it faced a large mirror that was carefully placed so subjects could not see their own reflections. They stared into "the depths of the mirror" as they waited for the departed to appear.

Time in the Apparition Room was precipitated by a day of relaxation, light meals, no caffeine, leisurely strolls, and sessions of reminiscing about the deceased people they hoped to see. Subjects were also encouraged to bring photos and personal items that had belonged to that person.

The results were astonishing. Dr. Moody reported that over 50 percent of subjects experienced contact with a ghost. Sometimes, however, it was not the targeted relative they wanted to see, but someone else who had played a part in their life. Some encounters were simply auditory while others did not occur until hours after the session in the Apparition Room.

Dr. Moody noted that the spirits who appeared were generally as solid as live human beings, yet looked years younger and more vibrant than they had in life.

Author's note: Some critics warn that exploration of a psychomanteum may be detrimental to the mental health of unstable people. Those who wish to experiment should first consult Dr. Moody's Web site for more information: www.lifeafterlife.com.

HAUNTED HOSPITALS

Hospitals are among the most haunted places on earth. Death, although common there, is usually nonviolent. Nonetheless, it can result in stubborn spirits who refuse to budge—even after the buildings leave medicine behind and become apartment houses, office complexes, and hotels, as they so often do.

The following cases explore encounters in the once-hushed halls where sick folks hoped to heal, yet sometimes succumbed to the all-too eager arms of death.

ROOM 611

When asked about his favorite investigation involving a ghost in the mirror, San Antonio, Texas's ghost hunter Martin Leal did not hesitate before naming a former hospital.

The skyscraper on East Houston Street was erected in 1928 as the

Medical Arts Building, and we can only imagine the drama that filled its fourteen floors in the five decades it served patients.

Though the one-time hospital is today the luxurious Emily Morgan Hotel, we cannot rule out the possibility that it collected at least one of its ghosts during its new incarnation. It is also likely that many of the restless spirits result from bygone days when so many people passed away within the hospital's walls.

"I have been investigating the Emily Morgan for eight years," said Martin, who is both a paranormal researcher and the creator and guide of San Antonio's popular Haunting History Tour. Hotel employees keep him updated on ghost sightings. The hotel, across the street from the notoriously haunted Alamo, is a favorite among ghost enthusiasts. Those in the know ask for room 611, according to Martin, who related the following story.

A woman attended a conference held at the Emily Morgan Hotel, trusting her secretary to make the reservations. Ghosts were the last thing on her mind when she checked into the hotel and accepted the key to room 611.

Around 9:00 p.m. the hotel's front desk clerk received a phone call from an alarmed guest. He listened to the muffled voice and thought that it sounded as if the excited woman was cupping her hand over her mouth to prevent someone else from hearing her. The clerk glanced down at the phone and saw that the call came from room 611.

"Help me!"

"Ma'am?" the clerk asked, concern in his voice.

"*Save me!*" the woman cried. "*There is a man in my room!*"

The clerk wasted no time. He sent two security guards to the rescue. They were prepared for the worst as they opened the door with a passkey. They cautiously stepped into the room and glanced around. The place appeared empty. They saw no intruder, let alone

Entities sometimes materialize in the mirrors of this former San Antonio, Texas, hospital. (Leslie Rule)

The architectural detail on this one-time hospital is exquisite. While some visitors are drawn to the building's beauty, others are intrigued by its ghosts. (Leslie Rule)

the frightened guest, until they noticed a woman peeking out from behind the curtains.

"There is a man over there!" she hissed and pointed to the bed. "*Get him!*"

The guards moved stealthily toward the bed and looked behind it. No one was there. Then they searched the room, checking out the closet and the bathroom.

"You can come out," they told the frightened woman. "There is no one here."

She was shaken as she emerged from her hiding place, her eyes darting around the room. "But he didn't leave!" She was bewildered. "I was watching and I would have seen him leave."

She explained to the security guards that she had been putting on makeup when she saw a man reflected in the mirror, standing behind her. She whirled around, but he was too fast for her. He had ducked behind something. She was terrified to walk past the bed where she feared he was hiding, so she grabbed the phone and called the front desk.

The guards met each other's eyes. *Should they tell her?* It was not the first time something odd had occurred in that room. They knew why the guest had not seen the man leave: He was a ghost. The hotel management, however, had warned employees not to talk about the ghosts. They were concerned that if word of the haunting got out that guests would be afraid.

One guard finally spoke. "Maybe it was your imagination," he offered in an effort to comfort the anxious lady.

It was the wrong thing to say. The woman knew she had not imagined the man. Her face reddened and she raised her voice. "I did *not* imagine it! I know what I saw!" As she argued with the guard, the other guard radioed for the manager, who promptly appeared.

He tried to placate the woman. "We know it wasn't your imagination," he told her, and then explained that she was occupying one of the hotel's most haunted rooms. She had not seen a flesh-and-blood intruder, he told her. *Her* intruder had been a ghost, manifesting in the mirror for a shadow of a moment before slipping away.

"It was kind of funny," Martin added. "Because they did not doubt that she was looking in the mirror when she spotted the ghost. She had been applying lipstick when she saw his reflection and she turned her head so fast that she left a lipstick mark from her mouth to her ear."

EMILY MORGAN HOTEL
705 E. Houston Street
San Antonio, Texas 78205
(210) 225-5100 ❧ (800) 784-1180
www.emilymorganhotel.com

HAUNTING HISTORY TOUR
www.bestsanantonioghosttours.com

PILL HILL THRILL

Thousands upon thousands of Seattle residents took their first breaths there. And thousands upon thousands took their *last* breath there. It is Seattle's First Hill, a place where so many of the city's hospitals are clustered that locals call it Pill Hill.

It is not surprising the area is haunted. The hospitals are old, and the ghosts of both patients and the doctors and nurses who treated them have been sensed by witnesses.

A medical technician told me of napping between shifts in a room of an old wing of one of the Pill Hill hospitals. He awoke when the door suddenly opened, light spilled in, and a nurse looked at him. He did not recognize her, but that fact didn't surprise him, for he knew instantly that they "worked different shifts."

Her shifts had ended long ago, probably before he was born. She was dressed in an old-time uniform, complete with the little white cap upon her head.

Ghosts of patients likely outnumber the nurses and doctors a thousand to one. Although many people who are terminally ill prepare themselves for death when they check into the hospital and cross over quickly and peacefully, others, according to parapsychologists, remain earthbound.

Psychic people often confide that they see many apparitions in hospital corridors, and that seems to be a likely place for ghosts to linger. *Sometimes,* however, when the spirits leave, they are not headed toward the proverbial light. *Sometimes* wayward ghosts travel through the lobby and out the front door to wander aimlessly through the streets.

Donna Anders, a Seattle, Washington, suspense novelist, may have met a phantom patient who took just such a detour. It was a mild afternoon in 2004 and she had just left a doctor's office on Pill Hill where she had had a routine checkup. When her cell phone rang as she drove down Minor Street, Donna immediately pulled over to the side of the road. "It was right in front of the Stimson-Green Mansion," she said, explaining that she had scrutinized the sidewalks for pedestrians as she parked the car.

Suddenly, a face peered at her through the passenger window. "I was startled because no one had been there just a second before," said Donna.

The stranger was an elderly woman with her hair hidden beneath the hood of her pink sweat suit. Her palms were pressed flat against the window, framing a frightened, milk-white face.

As Donna stared into the bright, panicked eyes, she too became panicked for the woman appeared to be trying to open the car door.

"I pulled away," Donna said. Her initial shock, however, quickly turned to curiosity. "I circled the block so I could go back and get a look at her," she admitted. Traffic was light and she made it back to the spot so quickly that she did not think the woman could have gone far. Yet, the lady in pink was gone. Donna scanned the sidewalks, but saw no nearby shops or doorways that the woman could have entered.

She was perplexed. Donna felt certain that the woman was not a street person, for she had been too clean and neat. It was odd that the lady vanished so quickly. And two other things struck Donna as strange. It looked as if the woman was fumbling to open the car door but her hands were as ineffectual as the foggy fingers of a phantom.

Yet, it is the woman's complexion that haunts Donna the most. "She was so pale. I've never seen anyone so pale. She was white as a ghost."

First Hill is situated just east of Pioneer Square, and was logged by Seattle's pioneers. Before it earned the nickname Pill Hill, it was dubbed Profanity Hill. For decades, the courthouse occupied an area where Harborview Hospital now sits, and folks were so exhausted walking uphill to court that they spewed profanities.

Today, land on Pill Hill is at such a premium that the administrators of Virginia Mason Hospital recently purchased an acre of land for the staggering sum of $20 million. Many decades ago the area was known for its inexpensive housing. Prior to that, however, the wealthy built their mansions there, including one called Castlemount, the home of the Haller family.

Before it was demolished in the 1940s, the 1883 mansion was known as the Ghost House. Although details of what happened there are lost to history, it is interesting to note that the mansion sat on Minor Street, not far from the spot where Donna Anders encountered the mysterious agitated woman.

Pill Hill may be crawling with ghosts from all different eras.

There is probably not a hospital on earth that has not entertained a ghost. Though not everyone can see the spirits who wander the long sterile corridors or linger in the operating room where a surgery took a fatal turn—*they are there.*

Whether shadowy figures, smoky phantoms, or full-fledged apparitions, ghosts take many forms and all of the above have been spotted in hospitals around the globe.

In the following story, a hospital employee meets an apparition more than once in the hallway of a typical American hospital.

ALL IN A DAY'S WORK

Though probably not any more haunted than the average hospital, the University of Michigan Hospital in Ann Arbor, Michigan, has its share of ghosts. While some members of the staff may have worked there for decades without so much as glimpsing a darting shadow or hearing a whispered good-bye, there are still a few sensitive employees who admit to having ghostly encounters.

Stacey Kotlarcyzk, twenty-four, comes from a family of sensitives who have had more than their share of paranormal experiences. Stacey is no exception. In 2005, she began working as a health information assistant, a job that required her to pick up and deliver medical records throughout the hospital. As she walked the halls, pushing a cart of files, she soon got used to the routine.

Shortly after she began working there, she was headed past the emergency room when she noticed a young man in the corridor, just outside the door. He wore the standard hospital gown, and blood poured from a wound on his forehead. She barely had time to absorb the image before he vanished. "I figured he was someone who died in the emergency room," she said matter-of-factly.

She began to ask fellow employees if they had seen ghosts, and a few admitted that they too had had encounters at the hospital.

Over a year later, on a quiet morning in March 2006, Stacey was making her rounds in the basement and suddenly began to shiver. "It was unnaturally cold," she told me, explaining that she had just picked up a file from one of the bottom-floor departments. She was organizing her cart when a chill went through her. It was then that she noticed someone. "I saw him out of the corner of my eye." She could not understand where the man had come from because the hallway had been empty just a moment before.

She turned to watch him as he walked away, his back to her. He was an older gentleman with stooped shoulders and white hair. He was dressed in street clothes and was obviously not an employee. Yet, there was no reason for a patient to travel the basement corridors.

"I thought he was lost," said Stacey, who decided to offer her assistance. As she took a step in his direction, the man suddenly turned and walked purposefully *through* the wall.

Stacey's jaw dropped. "I realized I had just seen a ghost," she said. "But he looked like a live person."

Later, she told her father about the ghost who had stepped into a solid wall. "My father is in construction and years ago he did some work at the hospital. He told me that there had been extensive remodeling in that area. At one time, there were doorways there that have been sealed up."

When the man was alive, he may have taken that very path. Maybe he worked in the hospital long ago, or maybe he died there.

The area where the elderly man materialized happens to be near the morgue. Perhaps he was a recently departed spirit who had said one last good-bye to his body before journeying into the beyond.

THE ICE PICK TOUR

"The noise level of the ward went down, 'incidents' were fewer, cooperation improved, and the wards could be brightened when curtains and flowerpots were no longer in danger of being used as weapons." Dr. Walter Freeman, writing with enthusiasm about the benefits of the lobotomy.

In recent years, administrators have attempted to make hospitals seem cheerful. The days of all-white interiors and matching uniforms for staff are gone. Sometime in the last several decades, someone realized that hospitals are scary enough without such stark ambience. Interior decorators were instructed to create calming, yet fun environments.

Today, it is common to find hospitals with brightly painted walls, whimsical art, and nurses in smocks with silly cartooned patterns.

While the positive decor reassures both patients and their families, it can't erase a simple fact: Hospitals can be places of pain and sadness. Deaths are common there, and grieving relatives walk the halls as the tragedies play out. The emotional residue is palpable and all the bright paint in the world cannot hide it.

Perhaps the pall is the heaviest in places where the mind was sick or was simply *treated* as if it were sick.

In today's world, people are open about their mental problems and speak freely about taking prescribed drugs such as Prozac or Paxil for depression and anxiety. Indeed, sometimes it seems almost trendy to have attention deficit disorder or anxiety attacks. The topic has made its way into many a cocktail party as people chat about their favorite medications—the ones that made them gain or lose weight, and the ones they plan to try.

Embarrassment has waned because educated folks understand that chemical imbalances are common and do not imply weakness of character or a dark spot on the soul.

But it was not always so.

Imagine living in a time when being depressed brought shame and there were no wonder pills to cure it. Imagine being whisked away to a mental ward after suffering an anxiety attack. Suddenly, you are locked in a room, and, *perhaps,* your arms are tied to your sides as strangers pry open your mouth to force you to take foul-tasting medicine.

When you do not respond favorably, you are kept for months, or *years*—or even for the rest of your life. Maybe you are treated to an "ice pick" lobotomy, a procedure where a sharp instrument pierces the brain, severing nerves, and changes the personality forever.

You are hidden away, an embarrassing secret to your loved ones who come to see you on the rare Sunday. If you did not start out severely mentally disturbed, the grim environment of the institution and the extreme treatments would surely make you insane.

It is no wonder that so many old mental institutions are haunted. For those who lived and died within the cold, gray walls of such places, are often especially restless.

The Northern State Hospital in Sedro-Woolley, Washington, is one such place. The institution, opened in 1912, is notoriously haunted and was home to droves of patients until the burden to taxpayers was deemed unnecessary and it was shut down in 1973.

Though often heralded as a kinder alternative to the "snake pit" asylums of yesteryear, there is no getting around the fact that not every patient received gentle treatment at Northern. The hospital was one of the stops on Dr. Walter Freeman's lobotomy tour. He traveled the country, performing the procedure he had perfected, and teaching it to other doctors in twenty-three states.

Patients with everything from a mild case of the blues to obsessive-compulsive disorder to schizophrenia received the treatment.

Archived records note that Dr. Freeman visited Northern State Hospital in June of 1949 during his trans-orbital phase. The trans-orbital lobotomy, invented by Dr. Freeman, was performed via the eyeball—and he was particularly proud of it.

Dr. Freeman performed thousands of lobotomies from 1936 to 1967 when his final procedure ended with a dead patient and he was banned from operating.

One of his most famous lobotomies was performed on poor Rosemary Kennedy in 1941. The twenty-three-year-old sister of future president John F. Kennedy was a spirited and somewhat slow young lady whose mood swings troubled her father. Without consulting his wife, Joe Kennedy signed his daughter up for the surgery. The lobotomy stole her personality, crippling her to the point that she was institutionalized until her death at age eighty-six in January 2005.

While the public eventually became aware of the tragic Kennedy case, the destruction of ordinary folks may have gone unnoticed. What became of those ruined people? Some eventually died on the premises from various ailments not directly attributed to their lobotomies.

For a number of years, much of the campus has remained vacant as the community whispers about troubled spirits.

I received a letter from someone who knows the hospital well. Years ago, she became familiar with the creak of each door, the length of each hall, and the wink of each dusty window that peered out into the night.

Jeannie Packer was just a teenager and the hospital had been vacant for years when Northern State Hospital became her playground. She explained in her letter that her father was superintendent there, and his job was to prepare the place so that other state agencies could utilize the small buildings.

Here is an excerpt from her letter:

When we arrived, Northern State had been a virtual ghost town for the better part of six years. During that time, the campus had sat untouched. There were still remnants laying about—furniture, paperwork, medical supplies, and yes, even patients' personal effects. It was an amazing time capsule.

I became fascinated with the campus from the first time I saw it. Even though it had been abandoned for several years, the buildings and grounds projected a majestic beauty. It was picturesque. And one could just feel all of the history lurking about.

I never believed in ghosts before I came to Northern State. In fact, I assumed that people who did were a little off in their heads. I was, however, proven very wrong.

In April of 1984, late on a Saturday night, I took my boyfriend (now my husband) and a couple of friends to Northern State. They had been curious about the campus because of all the bizarre things that had happened there while the hospital was running.

I took them to the old superintendent's mansion. I chose that building because, to be quite frank, it was isolated, and I felt sure that we would not be detected by the night security guard. The building was located in a section of campus that was not in use. When we arrived, it was about 11:30 p.m. This end of campus had no electricity, so a full moon and our flashlights were the only light. These buildings were too large and too expensive to heat. Basically, they were rotting.

I led my friends to the back door—an old servants' entrance—my usual way in. We turned on our flashlights and I gave them a tour. I showed them the kitchen, the back staircase that led to the third-story servants' quarters, and the dining room where a large chandelier lay on the floor. (At some point, thieves had tried to steal it, but it was too massive to fit through the doorways. It had been soldered piece by piece around 1920.) We walked through the study and the formal living room, which was once a ballroom. Finally, we began to climb the formal staircase. As we climbed the steps, both of our flashlights failed at the same instant and we noticed a faint light coming from the second floor. It did not make sense as there was no electricity.

We were not afraid yet, just curious. We continued up the stairs, and down the long hallway toward the light. We rounded a corner and the hallway was illuminated.

The light was coming from the master bedroom at the end of the hall. There, the light was so bright that it hurt our eyes. It was totally blinding, like looking into the sun.

The room was much colder than the rest of the house. Still, we were not scared—just utterly baffled. My friend tapped me on the shoulder and pointed. A chill went down my spine. The intense light seeped from the cracks around the closet door.

I had previously explored it, and knew it was just an ordinary walk-in closet. There was no sound, so we knew that a generator was not running.

The light was brighter than anything we had seen before. My husband wanted to open the door. The rest of us became totally freaked. He touched the doorknob and we ran.

As we raced down the hallway, the light vanished, leaving us in the dark. We ran, scared out of our wits in the pitch black.

My husband later told me that the instant we left the room, the light went out.

I had been in that house many times before that night, and never had a bit of trouble. But that night, there seemed to be a force at work.

I never again entered that house.

I can still feel the hair stand up on the back of my neck whenever I think about it. And as hard as I try, I've never come up with a plausible explanation.

Archives list countless cases of patients dying as a result of "maniac exhaustion" at Northern State. One account I stumbled upon tells of a death in the Skagit River as a desperate young man tried to escape the institution. On July 7, 1938, twenty-eight-year-old Charles Rytylahti tried to make his way across the river on a log when he fell into the water and drowned.

Much of the drama at the Northern State Hospital was not documented, and the memories remain only in the minds of the ghosts tethered to the crumbling buildings.

Spotlight on the Investigators

Darren Thompson, president of Washington Paranormal Research (WSPIR), cofounded the Seattle-based organization with his wife, Jill, who serves as director. Since its inception in April 2005, the nonprofit group's ranks have grown and today they count over sixty members who assist them in investigating more than twenty cases each year.

When asked to name the area's most haunted locations, Darren chose two places. Each was meant to be a place of healing, yet each had a history of abuse. It is probably that abuse that led to the haunting.

Northern State Hospital in Sedro-Woolley, Washington, is among the most active sites investigated by WSPIR. Today, Job Corp occupies part of the campus and Darren interviewed three employees there during a 2007 investigation. The witnesses, who include a Job Corp instructor, had all seen the apparition of a young girl.

Every encounter occurred in the daytime, and each happened in a different building. All described a ghostly girl who clutched a ball, and floated toward them before vanishing. The girl's identity remains a mystery. WSPIR has yet to find a death of a child documented at the site.

Members of WSPIR share a common goal and have two main focuses. "We want to help those who are experiencing paranormal activity, and are in fear," Darren said, explaining that the unknown in itself can be frightening, and that collecting data that sheds light on a haunting can alleviate panic.

The scientific examination of the data is also vital to WSPIR members who strive to carefully record information and note patterns.

For the Northern State Hospital investigation, the group was divided into five teams who took turns exploring the Denny Building. "The most remarkable experience was with one particular team," said Darren, who explained that members first heard footsteps behind them and then the sound of stones being tossed. Just as the team's psychic was sensing that past residents there had had financial worries, they heard the distinctive clink of a coin hitting the floor.

A member of the team felt something hit his back and when the others searched the floor, they found a breath mint.

The other location that WSPIR considers to be highly active is the site of one of the most shocking cases of medical abuse in state history. Olalla, Washington, on Puget Sound, was once home to Linda Burfield Hazzard, a nurse with limited training who, because of slack laws of the era, was allowed to practice medicine. Her unorthodox methods of healing resulted in agonizing death for some of her patients in the early 1900s.

The author of the book, *Fasting for the Cure of Disease*, Linda viewed fasting as the key to curing everything from blindness to arthritis and withheld food from her patients for months, feeding them only a broth made from tomatoes and asparagus tips, and an occasional teaspoon of orange juice. She also implemented digestive cleansing rituals that left her subjects screaming in agony.

Linda and her drunken, bigamist husband Sam Hazzard lived on a wooded site where they ran a sanitarium that locals dubbed "Starvation Heights."

While many of her patients were willing participants, others tried to escape. They were sometimes discovered by neighbors who were shocked at the sight of the withered beings with faces drawn and gaunt, their bones sharply outlined beneath thin skin as they hobbled down the road and begged for food.

Though dozens died while under her care, Linda Hazzard was punished for just one death. In 1912 she was convicted of manslaughter for starving

Claire Williamson, a wealthy Australian woman. After several years in the Walla Walla State Prison, she was pardoned and eventually went back to Olalla and continued starving patients until 1935 when her beloved sanitarium burned to the ground. In 1938, she succumbed to her own starvation treatment.

No one knows exactly how many people died on the property and it has long been suspected that some victims were secretly buried there.

The memory of the horrid ordeal faded with the past, and the folks who occupied the old Hazzard home were unaware of the case until recent years when an inquisitive journalist knocked on their door.

On a June evening in 2005 the residents allowed WSPIR team members to conduct an investigation. At the time, they told Darren that the ghost of a young boy had been seen by several people and was often observed by their two grade-school-aged sons.

"They told us that one of their sons was upset because the ghost boy wanted to play blocks," said Darren. "He wasn't upset because he'd seen a ghost. He was upset that the ghost wanted to play a lame game."

Another son was home sick when the spirit materialized beside him on the couch. The apparition laid his head back, and began to cry. "The ghost boy won't tell me what's wrong," the concerned child later told his parents.

Witnesses have also heard the sound of heavy boots clomping down the stairs and seen a lightbulb unscrewed by invisible hands.

No records have been found to indicate that a boy lived and died on the property, but Linda Hazzard had no qualms about children "taking the treatment."

Linda had once advised a mother of an infant to follow her instructions and both mother and child then starved to death.

While ghost investigations can be tedious, and visits to haunted locations uneventful, some of the evidence collected at Starvation Heights thoroughly spooked WSPIR members.

"We captured several class A EVPs at Starvation Heights," said Darren, referring to the term for phantom voices inexplicably recorded. The most startling of the phrases caught include:

"Help us."

"Are you talking about us now?"

"Dig us up."

Author's note: The former haunted home has been dismantled and ghosts are no longer seen on the property.

After WSPIR members appeared on a Seattle television talk show to discuss the haunting at Starvation Heights, the Olalla neighborhood was disturbed by trespassers. As a result, neighbors are intolerant of curious intruders and will not hesitate to call the police on outsiders who venture too close.

❧

Despite the fact that the following case involves a place once known as a school, it was not a normal place of learning.

First occupied by the Halloran General Hospital in 1942, the institution served injured war heroes. Later, however, when it was known as a school, sick people lived on the premises. Ironically, most were healthy before they arrived and were made sick by the doctors.

WILLOWBROOK

Jennifer Vinciguerra does not mind working alone in the one-story, U-shaped building that sits on a sprawling campus in Staten Island, New York. As a social worker, she has seen the living do all sorts of strange things, and she is not fazed by the behavior of the dead.

Although others are frightened by the sounds and sights seen and heard after hours, Jennifer isn't. "I'm not afraid, but my coworker doesn't want to be there alone. If she sees that I am leaving, she leaves too."

Today, the state agency that occupies Jennifer's building serves the developmentally disabled, and she and the others are trained to treat all clients with respect—but this was not always so.

At one time, the entire campus was the site of the Willowbrook State School, where challenged children and adults lived and sometimes died. "We are required to watch documentaries about Willowbrook as part of our training," said Jennifer, explaining that administrators hope to prevent future cruelty in institutions by teaching social workers about the atrocities of the past.

Jennifer was horrified to learn that the staff at the overcrowded institution forced people to take group showers. "They rounded them up and hosed them down," she said. She was more shocked by the Willowbrook Hepatitis Study, where children at the facility were purposefully infected with the disease. The controversial program began in the mid-1950s and continued into the early 1970s.

When the public eventually learned of the practice, they were outraged, charging that the children were guinea pigs and that the doctors used them to study the progression of hepatitis and test unproven and harmful vaccinations. The institution's director, however, claimed that the children were doomed to become infected by living in the unsanitary environment and that they were better off contracting the disease under the doctors' control.

The children, of course, had no voice in the matter. Maybe that is why some of them still linger today.

The Willowbrook State School once inhabited the numerous buildings on the land and today those structures are used for a variety of purposes. While many of the buildings have been absorbed by a college campus, Jennifer's agency occupies one building. "It was once the children's ward," she said.

During the day, the place is filled with clients and staff. "I often stay late, but everyone else is gone by 4:30 p.m."

Everyone but the ghosts.

Sometimes as the sun slides behind the horizon and the shadows deepen, footsteps echo in the corridor outside of Jennifer's office. She and her coworker quickly open the door, but when they peer out, they see only an empty hallway.

"I was in the restroom when I heard what sounded like two children giggling," said Jennifer, adding that the toilets often flush by themselves when there is no one near the motion detectors.

Employees have also heard disembodied voices calling their names. Once, as Jennifer was walking through the lunchroom after hours, she was startled to hear a female voice clearly speak her name. At first, she thought that someone else had stayed late so she quickly searched the building only to discover she was all alone.

Jennifer, who is fascinated by the paranormal, confided, "I don't scare very easily but sometimes I get creeped out."

Those who haunt the former ward seem to be benign yet mischievous spirits.

A fellow employee once told Jennifer that she had seen the ghosts of two children in the building. "She saw them in the hallway from a distance," Jennifer said. "She saw a boy and a girl in dated clothing."

The woman was puzzled because their offices serviced *adults*. She could not figure out what the children were doing there so she followed them and watched as they turned the corner, disappearing from sight. When she peeked around the corner and saw the empty hallway, she realized she had just seen two ghosts.

When Jennifer heard the story, she was envious for she had always wanted to see a ghost. When she finally *did* encounter one, she did not realize it until months later.

One day as she steered her car into campus, she noticed a man standing in a clearing on the large sylvan lawn. She figured that the fellow must be one of the agency's developmentally disabled clients. Outsiders rarely venture onto the property, though joggers favor the mile-long road that loops around the campuses. But this man was definitely *not* a jogger. "It was very, very odd to see him out of context," she said.

The spot was isolated and some distance from the offices. And oddly, the man looked as if he had stepped right out of the 1970s. He was middle-aged and disheveled, with shaggy, gray hair and he wore a button-down shirt with an oversized collar.

Jennifer, who had worked in the building since 2004, had never seen anyone in that area so she studied the man carefully as she drove slowly by.

"He was so *still*," she remembered. "He did not move at all." He seemed to stare right through her and she had the sense that he did not see her.

"I decided to keep an eye out for him," she said, explaining that she was so curious that she vowed to find out more about him.

Though hundreds of clients are serviced at the agency, Jennifer has a sense of who comes and goes and she is sure if he was a client there that she would have seen him again. But six months have gone by and there has been no sign of the man.

Was he a ghost left over from an inhumane era?

We will never know the full extent of the indignities suffered by the residents of the Willowbrook State School. Advocates for humane treatment do not want the mean times to be forgotten.

And apparently, neither do the ghosts.

Haunted Hospitals

IN THE NEWS

Face in the Window

An abandoned hospital in Maysville, Kentucky, piqued the interest of ghost enthusiasts across the nation when a video of an apparition was captured there, according to the October 22, 2007, issue of Maysville's *Ledger Independent*.

The image, recorded by a startled, anonymous Lexington, Kentucky, resident, was caught in the spring of 2006 and gained a huge audience after it was shown on numerous Web sites and *The Maury Povich Show* pledged to air it.

Ghost researchers flocked to Maysville after viewing the milky form on the video. The figure appears to be looking out of a window on one of the Hayswood Hospital's upper floors. According to staff writer Misty Maynard, the form seems to morph from a smoky shape into a face with distinctive features and then leaps back from the window and vanishes.

The videographer was inspired to investigate the hospital after hearing of paranormal activity there. Some claimed they saw the ghost of a doctor and others heard the cries of a phantom baby.

Immortally Wounded

The September 1, 2006, issue of *Peterborough Today* reported that the Peterborough Museum in England is haunted by the ghost of an Australian soldier.

According to the account, the building was once a hospital where a wounded soldier took his last breath in June 1916. Ghost sightings of the young man date back to 1931 when the wife of the museum's caretaker, Mrs. Yarrow, came face-to-face with the spirit on the stairs. The man appeared so solid that Mrs. Yarrow at first assumed he was a visitor to the museum. The apparition was clad in a green suit, and the sound of his steps was unnaturally loud, a peculiar detail because the fellow was floating up the stairs.

The startled woman watched as the ghost walked through a closed door and down the hallway and then vanished.

The Peterborough Museum celebrated its seventy-fifth anniversary in 2006, and the ghost is still restless. Witnesses have felt the touch of ice-cold hands, and the museum staff have frequently arrived in the morning to find the furniture inexplicably rearranged.

Violent Eviction

"Demolition May Knock Ghosts Out of Old Hospital." That was the headline for the online edition of a news story from Cleveland, Ohio's, *WEWS News Five* on July 20, 2006. According to the account, ghost hunters were intrigued by phantom voices emanating from an abandoned mental hospital in Broadview Heights, Ohio.

Mayor Glenn Goodwin, however, denied access to three different groups of paranormal investigators who hoped to explore the interior of the Broadview Development Center before it was ground to dust.

An accompanying photograph showed the wrecking ball swinging toward the historic 1939 building, which had sat empty since 1989.

Author's note: Stories circulating about the ghosts include an undocumented sighting of the "Pink Lady," said to be a former patient. Despite the fact that the hospital faces the city's police station, the folks affiliated with the forgotten Ohio Web site somehow managed to sneak in and explore the spooky structure. They posted their fascinating photos online. The images depict artifacts such as patients' beds and empty bottles that once contained thorazine, a powerful drug used to treat those who are psychotic.

My research also revealed that a civil suit for wrongful death was filed in 1989 (the same year the hospital shut down), and named the administrator, Paul Shelling, as the defendant. The suit asked for $20,000 in damages. A settlement was reached in 1991.

3

Ghosts on the Road

When it comes to ghosts in the great outdoors, our highways are among the most haunted locations. Millions drive our freeways, cruise our boulevards, and putter along our country roads. Most make it to their destinations, yet a few take deadly detours.

In the following case a frightening freak accident made a city cry. One driver, however, was still spinning his wheels long after his family laid him to rest.

The Last Bus Stop

As Juanita Johnson drove down the freeway toward Lake City, Florida, she glanced at her side-view mirror and saw the reflection of a bus, traveling in the fast lane. It was a ways behind her, but close enough for her to recognize the distinctive red, white, and blue colors of a Greyhound bus.

It did not occur to her that the bus might be following her. And it certainly did not occur to her that the bus was anything other than a diesel-powered vehicle with a live human being behind the wheel.

Juanita's sister, Becky, sat beside her in the rented two-toned Thunderbird, and her sister's three kids were in the backseat. It was a June day in 1980 and the group was on the first leg of a much-anticipated road trip to visit relatives in Little Rock, Arkansas.

Juanita was a nervous driver and she was glad to have handwritten directions from a man who knew these roads. He had assured her that the route was safe. But whenever she glanced at the sheet of paper with the neatly printed directions, she felt a surge of sadness.

❧

A few weeks earlier, Juanita had boarded a Greyhound bus near her home in Tampa, Florida, and smiled at Mike, the friendly driver. She often took the bus to her job at Martin's Uniform Company in St. Petersburg where she was district manager. She had gotten to know the bus driver well enough to ask him to sample a new line of trousers the company was trying out. "We gave Mike five pairs so he could tell us if they were comfortable on long drives," Juanita explained.

She always felt safe and secure with Mike at the wheel. "He was conscientious. He checked the mirrors often and was very aware of the traffic around us," she said. "I usually took the bus in bad weather. I didn't like to drive in the rain." It was nice to know she was in good hands on those days that the torrential Florida rains hit.

Mike soon became aware of how nervous she was whenever they drove over the Howard Franklin Bridge. The bridge was several miles long and spanned the Tampa Bay, connecting Tampa to St. Petersburg.

"Our company had supplied uniforms to firefighters who had had an accident on the Howard Franklin Bridge and I had been afraid to ride over it ever since," Juanita confided.

Whenever the Greyhound bus reached the last stop before they crossed the bridge, Mike would turn to her with a nod of warning. "He'd tell me that it was time to go to the back of the bus and look over my paperwork," she said.

Juanita would sit in one of the last rows of the bus, smoke a cigarette, and study her papers to distract herself from the metallic hum of the bridge beneath the wheels.

One day when she boarded the bus in early May, Juanita asked Mike for advice about her upcoming vacation. "I was scared about driving over the mountains, and I wanted to know the safest route," she told me.

Soon after, Mike stopped by the uniform office and gave her handwritten directions. Juanita thought it was a very kind gesture. She knew that Mike and his wife had been through a recent heartbreaking loss. "Another driver told me that they had moved to Florida from the New York area after they lost a child in an accident," said Juanita.

Despite his own troubles, Mike took the time to help others and seemed especially concerned with the safety and comfort of his passengers.

On the morning of May 9, 1980, Juanita took the Greyhound bus to work and said good-bye to Mike at her stop in St. Petersburg. About an hour later she was seated at her desk when she received a disturbing phone call from a fellow employee.

"Thank God you're ok!" the woman cried when she heard Juanita's voice. "We were afraid that you were on the bus that went into the bay!"

❧

Bridges are a fact of life in Florida. They crisscross the gulfs and bays, rising high above the water for the millions of commuters who travel over the many waterways.

While Juanita's trip across the Howard Franklin Bridge that morning had been uneventful, it was not the last bridge on the Greyhound's Miami-bound route. Not long after Juanita got off at her stop in St. Petersburg, Mike continued southbound onto the Sunshine Skyway Bridge.

With a five-and-a-half-mile span, it is the longest bridge in the world, connecting Pinellas to Bradenton over the Tampa Bay. On a sunny day, the view from the bridge is exhilarating, with the wide expanse of ocean glistening below.

On this morning, however, fog closed in, the rain slammed down as the wind whipped the water below, and the view abruptly vanished. Drivers could not see beyond their own windshields as a tropical storm hit.

Mike knew that his twenty-eight passengers were counting on him to keep them safe, so he slowed down and turned on his fog lights.

The conditions were treacherous and they were about to get worse.

For 150 feet below the bridge, the captains of a massive freighter were also struggling to navigate through the storm. As the fog moved over the helm of the SS *Summit Venture*, the captains could barely see past the wheel of the 608-foot-long ship.

The vessel was bound for a Tampa dock where workers were prepared to load 28,000 tons of phosphate aboard for transport to the Orient, but the freighter was temporarily empty and rode high in the wild, dark water. The fifty-plus miles an hour squall forced the ship off course as the disoriented captains fought for control. Still, they believed that they were headed toward the immense gap between the bridge's support piers.

As the bus crept over the Sunshine Skyway Bridge, the ship's captains glimpsed something that would loom in their nightmares for the rest of their lives. A bridge abutment blocked their way.

It was 7:38 a.m. when the near 2,000-ton vessel slammed into the southern bridge piling. A quarter-mile section of the steel bridge collapsed, sending eight cars and the Greyhound bus plummeting into the bay.

The top of the bus was sheared off, and the shocked witnesses of the aftermath likened it to the lid ripped from a tin can. Thirty-five people died, most from the impact of the 150-foot fall, while a few survived the drop, only to drown. The lone survivor was a young man in a pickup truck that landed on the ship.

Juanita was numb as she read the newspaper, shocked by the tragic loss of life of the friendly bus driver, his passengers, and the poor people in the cars. She could not stop her tears when the TV news reporters told of the rescuers' long and arduous effort to recover the victims from the twisted metal of the bridge.

"My heart was heavy," she told me. She felt so sad for Mike's wife and all of the others who had lost loved ones.

A few weeks later when she embarked on her June trip to Little Rock, armed with Mike's directions, she still could not shake the sorrow. "I did not know him well, but he was a special person and I felt immense sadness over the tragedy," she said.

That should have been the end of it. It did not occur to Juanita that the kind bus driver would ever play a role in her life again.

Yet from the moment she glanced at her side-view mirror and saw the reflection of the bus she sensed something strange. It wasn't that she thought it was a phantom bus. That would have been a ludicrous assumption. She simply found it odd that it stayed framed in her mirror for so many miles. "I kept expecting it to pass," she said. For nearly an hour, almost every time she glanced in the side-view mirror, there was the Greyhound bus in the fast lane, always the same distance behind her, even when she slowed.

When she pulled off at the truck stop in Lake City, Florida, she watched the freeway for a moment, waiting for the bus. "I knew a few of the Greyhound bus drivers so I was curious to see whose bus it was," she said. Traffic on the freeway whizzed by with no sign of the bus.

"I figured it turned off somewhere, so I wasn't fazed," said Juanita. She filled up her tank, and the group headed toward Little Rock where they had a fun but uneventful time until their return days later.

"The rental car was a lemon," Juanita said. "Everything went wrong." The Thunderbird broke down a couple of times, the air in the tires was low, and they were rear-ended by teenagers who took off. "The taillight was broken and we tried to turn the car in for another one, but it didn't work out. We passed several accident scenes, including one where an eighteen-wheeler was on its side. We were exhausted at the end of the trip," she said. "It was about 3:00 a.m. and we were on I-10. Becky was driving and we had just come off the Mobile to Pensacola Bridge when a storm hit."

Becky's young daughters, Angie and Martizall, and Juanita's son, Timmy, were asleep in the backseat. Juanita, her fourteen-year-old daughter Kimberly, and Becky were all trying to stay alert.

The steady patter of the rain and the rhythmic beat of the windshield wipers were dangerously soothing. Juanita glanced at her sister's nodding head and warned, "Becky, don't fall asleep!"

Becky jerked her head up and tried to watch the road, but soon her eyelids were heavy. Juanita, was also nodding off when the inside of the car was illuminated by the headlights of the vehicle behind them.

"He'd better get off my tail!" Becky cried, suddenly alert.

"Where did he come from?" Juanita asked as she twisted around in her seat to see a bus tailgating them. It followed them closely for awhile, its glaring headlights rudely flooding the Thunderbird's interior.

"What's he doing on my bumper?" Becky was annoyed.

Finally, it cut around them and as it passed, Becky, Juanita, and Kimberly saw the logo of the long white dog stretched across the side. It was a Greyhound bus.

The three were wide awake as they watched the taillights of the bus as it gained speed and drove ahead. "It was a long, straight stretch of road," said Juanita, explaining that they could observe the taillights from a distance. After a few moments, they saw the bus pull off to the side of the road.

"Look, it pulled over!" said Juanita. "I wonder if it's having trouble."

"I'm not stopping to help a bus!" Becky said firmly, now alert and feisty.

As they came abreast of the stalled bus, Becky and Juanita turned to look at it. And then the oddest thing occurred. As they stared at the big bus with the dog on the side, the image melted. The bus vanished and in its place was a small van.

"Did you see *that*?" Juanita cried.

Their adrenaline pumping, Juanita and Becky questioned each other about what they had seen. There was no doubt. The Greyhound bus had been there and it had dissolved before their eyes.

After the shock, they couldn't have fallen asleep even if they tried. They remained alert and aware for the rest of the way home.

Nearly thirty years later, Juanita's daughter, Kimberly Bruklis, also remembers the treacherous trip. "I was only fourteen when it happened," she said. "But I remember clear as day the leaping Greyhound dog on the side of the massive bus as it went by and I remember all the commotion afterward when they saw the bus transform."

Juanita was so puzzled by the experience that she contacted the Greyhound station to ask which one of their buses was on that route but she didn't mention the ghostly bus. The answer was chilling. Greyhound had no buses on that stretch, during that time.

The bus was a phantom, zooming down the road where Mike had once driven his Greyhound bus—the route he had promised would be safe for Juanita's family.

"Becky was almost asleep at the wheel," Juanita remembered, her voice filled with awe. "If it hadn't been for the bus, we could have been in an accident. We could have been killed. It was as if Mike was our guardian angel."

The implications are huge and uplifting. The spirit of a man killed in one of the country's worst bridge accidents lingered on earth to save the life of a passenger.

Twenty-eight passengers went down with the bus, and if there was time for emotion, the conscientious Greyhound driver surely felt regret. Warranted or not, he may have felt guilt. And he may have thought of the one passenger, so terrified of bridges, who planned to follow his directions for a trip that could become dangerous.

Many believe that those who die gain an incredible sense of "knowing" in the afterlife and can foresee things to come. If this is true, Mike knew that Becky would fall asleep at the wheel and that her family was in danger.

In one last kind gesture, Michael Curtin saved the lives of five people.

❧

Sometimes, as we travel down the road, we catch a glimpse of a moment long gone. Perhaps we see a snippet of the past so ordinary that we don't stop to question it. For instance, who would give much thought to a group of pedestrians waiting at the crosswalk for the light to change?

Though the people may be long dead, we'd never think that they were anything but flesh and blood, breathing beings unless they vanished before our eyes—*or* if they beat us to the next block despite the fact that they were on foot and we were in fast-moving traffic.

Sometimes this happens with roadside ghosts. I once corresponded with a woman who had this type of recurring roadside encounter. One night, she and her husband were driving along a quiet stretch of highway. They passed an older man in a beige overcoat who stood on the side of the road beside an automobile with its hood up. They continued by and did not think much of the scene until they'd traveled perhaps another eighth of a mile and saw him *again*. The same man stood on the roadside, in the same beige overcoat, beside a car that was identical to the first, also with its hood up.

After the woman and her husband witnessed the anomaly, they grilled each other for details just to be certain that they had seen the same thing.

How could the man and his immobilized vehicle appear in both spots just seconds apart? There is no answer that fits within the guidelines of conservative rules of time and space.

The couple concluded they had seen a ghost.

If they had not seen the fellow twice, it would never have occurred to them that he was anything other than an ordinary man with car trouble.

When the scene takes on a morbid twist, however, witnesses are more likely to have questions, especially when the "people" seen are dressed in dated clothing.

Anita Scheftner had such an encounter, and it was so startling that it stays with her as clearly as if it were yesterday, despite the fact that nearly three decades have passed.

It was April 1979, she explained. Anita and her husband were living in Waterville, Maine, and had just become new parents. They often took Sunday drives with their infant daughter, Wendy, and marveled at the beauty of the New England scenery.

As the young family traveled along a country road, enjoying a spring day, Anita noticed something odd by the side of the road. A small cluster of people in Colonial dress were engaged in a cruel task. The men were piling rocks upon a person who lay beneath a sheet of wood. "I thought that they were acting out for a Colonial days festival," Anita explained. "As gruesome as that sounds, it was the only thing that made sense."

As they drove past the peculiar scene, Anita cried, "Did you see that?"

"See what?" asked her surprised husband.

"Those people were putting rocks on someone!" she said.

Though her husband was focused on driving, Anita thought that he should have noticed the activity. The people, after all, *were* on his side of the car. But he hadn't seen anything—only grass and trees.

They turned the car around and went back.

Though only a moment had passed, there was no trace of the scene Anita had witnessed. She knew that centuries earlier people in the area were sometimes crushed to death as punishment. She had read about Giles Corey, the elderly seventeenth-century man accused of witchcraft, who had been executed in that manner in Massachusetts.

Had such a horror once taken place beside the quiet country road in Maine? Had Anita been treated to a macabre peek into the past?

Though she does not have the answers, Anita will always remember the strange scene she glimpsed from a car window.

The following are more cases of ghosts on the road.

Ghost Crossing

According to paranormal author and psychic Susan Sheppard, it is not just buildings that harbor ghosts. In her list of *13 Places Most Likely to Be Haunted*, she states that crossroads are, "places of great spiritual power."

The creator of the award-winning Haunted Parkersburg Ghost Tours in Parkersburg, West Virginia, theorizes that intersections may disrupt the energy of a given location. While researching haunted spots, Susan recommends that paranormal investigators gather EVP and photographs in the vicinity of two intersecting roads to increase their chances of gathering impressive data.

Susan also points out that tunnels, too, are notoriously haunted, adding, "Just about all tunnels have ghosts." She speculates that tunnels can trap the energy of spirits but cautions that they may appear more active than they actually are because of the dark and spooky ambience.

HATE ON HAIGHT

Haight-Ashbury.

It may be the most famous intersection in America. Two ordinary green street signs mark the California corner that was the heart of the hippie haven in the 1960s.

Janis Joplin, Jefferson Airplane, and the Grateful Dead were among the famous rockers who lived and frolicked in the San Francisco district that is synonymous with the Summer of Love. The 1967 movement beat with the pulse of young people throughout America.

Free spirits roamed "the Haight," an approximate six-square block area bordered by Golden Gate Park. They attended free concerts on

Hippie Hill in the park. They let their hair grow, danced barefoot, and wore peace sign pendants. They dropped LSD, questioned authority, and preached love.

After four decades, some have passed on. Others are senior citizens, most long ago turned their ideals in for nine-to-five jobs. And some are ghosts, stuck in a groove like repeating drumbeats on a warped record album.

The district now caters to tourists who wander through the hip coffee shops and rows of stores that sell tie-dyed T-shirts, strawberry incense, and black-light posters.

Though the Summer of Love has faded like a pair of blue jeans left in a washing machine full of bleach, throngs visit the Haight to remember and honor the era. And some visit to hear about, and perhaps glimpse, the earthbound spirits who remain.

"The area is totally haunted," Tommy Netzband told me. He is the creator and guide of the Haunted Haight Walking Tour, and is well aware of the fact that love was not the only emotion promoted there.

Hate, too, played a part and all of the bumper stickers in the world could not obliterate it. Charles Manson, the crazed cult leader who persuaded his followers to commit mass murder, spent time in the Haight, with some accounts alleging that he lived at 616 Page Street.

Over the years, many were victims of crime in the area. Sadly, an innocent teenager was caught in the crosshairs of hate at the intersection of Haight and Ashbury.

"People still hear him running," said Tommy, who took me to the fatal corner one chilly fall night. He showed me the spot where the victim's blood had stained the sidewalk decades ago. "I deliberately don't tell people what happened here," he said, explaining that he waits to see if anyone will sense the energy before he shares the tragic story.

"I've had a number of people tell me that they hear the sound of running footsteps just as we are walking down the hill," he said. The phantom footfalls trace the same path the teenager took as he ran for his life. "Some people have trouble breathing here," he added, explaining that sensitive folks on his tour may empathize with the victim so much that they experience the anxiety of his last moments. He pointed to a house across the street. "A candle maker lived there. When he saw the kid running by, he shot him from the doorway."

Tommy, a longtime resident of the Haight, is also the founder of the San Francisco Ghost Society and is well versed in theories pertaining to the paranormal. He raises the possibility that the spirit of the youth has moved on, and that the activity is the result of a "residual haunting." In other words, the boy's soul is free but his energy left an imprint on the intersection.

In addition to collecting ghost stories, Tommy also delves into the history of the Haight to authenticate the cases. My own research confirmed Tommy's information. A February 1969 edition of the *San Francisco Chronicle* reported that police had arrested two candle makers suspected of shooting a teenager on February 26.

Robert J. Robinson, twenty-four, and Loren Morell, twenty-three, of 648 Ashbury Street were questioned in the death of seventeen-year-old Larry Watts. The suspects were white and the teenager was black. As Larry ran down the street with two friends at about 5:15 p.m., witnesses heard a man shout, "Hey you, stop!"

Bullets from a 30-30 rifle struck Larry and he died instantly.

In my quest to verify the horror on Haight and Ashbury, I unearthed another account of a death at the very intersection. The fatalities occurred thirty-five years apart *to the day*.

On February 26, 1934, Mary E. van Detton, a seventy-five-year-old retired postal worker crashed into the side of a railway car on

Haight and Ashbury. She was rushed to the hospital but died before she could be treated.

The coincidences continued. In addition to the victims' rhyming names, both Mary and Larry lived on the 1500 block. Mary lived at 1526 Haight Street (next door to the future home of musician Jimi Hendrix) and Larry at 1517 Eighth Avenue.

Shirts silhouetted in a store window resemble headless apparitions as they stare out onto the tragic corner of Haight and Ashbury. (Leslie Rule)

It also seems odd that a major player in each death shared initials along with similar sounding names. *Loren Morell*, his candle-making partner's accomplice, was arrested on the run with the gun in his trunk. *Leonard Moore* drove the fatal railway car that collided with Mary.

Yet *another* article surfaced about a man with a similar name who crashed his car on the next block up, on the intersection of Page and Ashbury. On August 28, 1910, Thomas *Morrow's* automobile collided with a trolley and the impact scattered the car's passengers over the street. Sixteen-year-old Emily Scott was seriously injured. A bystander carried her to a hospital a block away where she regained consciousness several hours later.

In the telling of the Morrow account, the *Chronicle* noted that the location had been dubbed "Death Hill," because of all the accidents there. As of this writing, however, my searches have failed to turn up more details about violence or accidents between Page and Haight on Ashbury, and I do not know if Emily Scott survived the car wreck. Let's hope that she lived a long and happy life. The district has plenty of ghosts without her.

For a corner associated with peace and love, Haight-Ashbury has a horrifying history. It is no wonder it is haunted.

www.hauntedhaight.com

Haunted Highways

Credible witnesses have reported seeing ghosts around the world on freeways, tunnels, bridges, and quiet country roads.

Here are a few roadways where the spirits of the dead still linger.

Golden Gate Ghosts

One of the most famous bridges in America, San Francisco's Golden Gate Bridge, is also one of the most haunted, according to Tommy Netzband of the San Francisco Ghost Society.

*   "Over 1,300 people have committed suicide by leaping off of the bridge since it opened in 1937," he said, adding that he believes many regretted the fatal choice the instant they began to fall.

The disembodied screams of the dead have been heard by many witnesses, who most often report hearing the shrieks late at night.

In addition to suicide victims, twenty-four workers died during the four-year construction of the bridge. "Two men fell into the wet cement during construction," said Tommy. Legend has it that the victims remain entombed in the pier, though highway officials dispute that claim.

Members of the San Francisco Ghost Society have heard reports of ghostly activity around this famous yet tragic bridge. (Leslie Rule)

Rarely included in the thousands of published photographs of the famous landmark, historic Fort Point sits at the foot of the Golden Gate Bridge. Some say that the lost spirits of the bridge victims seek refuge on the grounds of the fort, which was built by U.S. Army engineers and completed in 1861.

Over one thousand people have ended their lives within screaming distance of this historic fort. (Leslie Rule)

Some tourists hope to spot spirits when they visit San Francisco's historic Fort Point. (Leslie Rule)

Do the shadows hide secrets in Fort Point? (Leslie Rule)

Fort Point is both beautiful and spooky. (Leslie Rule)

Do spirits rest on this bench within a San Francisco landmark? (Leslie Rule)

Erected to guard the harbor from attack during times of war, Fort Point has never been involved in battle but has seen its share of sadness in the shadow of the tragic bridge.

"We've also had reports of a ghost ship beneath the Golden Gate Bridge," Tommy told me. The vessel sails past Fort Point and vanishes.

Many people are surprised to learn that Fort Point was built before the Golden Gate Bridge. (Leslie Rule)

(415) 556-1693 (visitor information)
www.nps.gov

Fort Point is open to the public. It is located at the south anchorage of the Golden Gate Bridge, at the end of Marine Drive on the Presidio of San Francisco.

Doorways seem to open into forever inside of Fort Point. (Leslie Rule)

Keeler's Corner

A boy's ghost was seen by a startled driver in Lynnwood, Washington, on an early autumn morning on Keeler's Corner. He appeared to be about ten years old and was wearing knickers and an old-time cap.

The distinct yet transparent apparition stood on the outer edge of the three-lane highway by the old gas station. The figure materialized around the same time that nearby buildings were being demolished and he may have had a connection to the old structures.

Tragic Bride

The spirit of a murdered bride in Moscow appears at the entry to the city of Novorossijsk, where she has been seen by numerous witnesses and was reportedly photographed by a teenage girl with a cell phone camera.

The ghost is believed to be a young woman who was killed at her wedding in the 1950s. A jealous suitor stabbed the frightened woman to death.

The apparition can be seen wandering forlornly near the Seven Winds Pass.

THE HAUNTED
TRAVELER

Haunted travel is becoming an increasingly popular hobby for thrill seekers who will journey great distances for the chance to encounter ghosts.

Managers of hotels, bed and breakfasts, and restaurants who were once secretive about the entities that share their establishments now realize that ghosts can be good for business. For each customer who is frightened away by the thought of ghosts, there are at least three others who relish the idea of spending some time with them.

People headed for haunted hot spots are sometimes surprised to find the journey more exciting than the actual destination. For spirits may often materialize *along the way*, and catch them off guard.

Ports, depots, and terminals are among the most haunted places on earth. They contain tremendous amounts of energy, left by the millions of folks who have traveled through.

Whether it is the mournful whistle of a departing train or the thunderous roar of a landing plane, the sounds evoke emotion. It might be that of a loved one leaving forever, or of an old friend coming home. It does not matter, the feeling is intense.

All intense feelings add to a haunting and that alone might be enough to texture a place with palpable energy. But when you add accidents to the mix, you have a recipe for ghosts. Though thankfully rare, accidents are eventually associated with almost every port and depot in the world. When the accidents are fatal, ghosts may join the throngs.

In the following case, however, it is not an accident, but a purposeful violent act that may be the leading factor responsible for many of the ghosts who haunt the area.

TRAGIC FACES

Washing windows is a routine task, but the cleaning woman on the second floor of the Union Station in Kansas City, Missouri, found it anything but routine. When she scrutinized the glass for smudges, she was shocked to see a man's face peering back at her.

"She was on the second floor," said Becky Ray, a member of a small group of paranormal investigators who operate in the area. "There was no way anyone could be looking in at her."

The face was not *outside* the window; it was a reflection in the glass. But it was not her face. She whirled around and saw she was still alone.

At the request of staff at the station, Becky and her team conducted an investigation in October 2005. The nonprofit group has a dozen active members and has been involved in over one hundred investigations since they formed in 2003.

When Becky Ray was asked to name her top all-time haunted Missouri location, she did not hesitate. "It's the Union Station," she told me. The station opened on October 30, 1914, and is a grand work of architecture with its massive arched windows, ninety-five-foot-high ceiling, and enormous sparkling chandeliers.

With nearly a century to gather ghosts, the train station certainly has its share and both passengers and workers have seen strange things and experienced supernatural phenomena. The station employees were excited about sharing their stories with the paranormal researchers. Many had seen a woman in a black dress, reminiscent of the 1940s. "She is blond and she is seen walking down the stairs," said Becky, explaining that in the glamour days of train travel, the area was designated for women passengers who showered downstairs.

The team set up their usual equipment, including the standard electromagnetic field detectors, digital tape recorders, and a couple of video cameras. They pointed a camera at the very window where

The Kansas City Union Station is mirrored in the fountain on an autumn night. (Leslie Rule)

This ornate train station is one of Missouri's most haunted spots. (Leslie Rule)

the cleaning woman had encountered the face. A short while later, an astonished team member glanced at the monitor to see a face on the window and called the others over. While the phantom face appeared on the monitor, the team could not see it on the actual window. "It appeared for about ten minutes and then faded," said Becky, who was one of five witnesses to the phenomenon.

She took one look at the ghostly bearded face and tried to laugh it off. "I was sure that it had to be an illusion. I thought maybe we were seeing the reflection of a poster," she said, emphasizing that she is skeptical by nature. Despite a thorough search, she found no logical explanation.

They concluded that the face belonged to a ghost, and they suspected they knew who he was. He was Frank Nash—both killer and victim and the reason for the Kansas City Massacre.

Frank Nash was a member of the notorious Al Spencer Gang, criminals who terrorized Oklahoma in the 1920s. The law caught up

Some say that ghosts play in this train station restaurant. (Leslie Rule)

The spirit of the historic train depot is right at home with artifacts from the past. (Leslie Rule)

with him but couldn't hold him. He escaped from a federal prison in Leavenworth, Kansas, in October 1930.

After a nationwide manhunt and nearly three years on the run, he was finally apprehended in Hot Springs, Arkansas, in June 1933. Three officers transported the prisoner by train, and arrived in Kansas City at 7:15 a.m. on June 17.

A car was waiting to take Nash back to prison. Seven lawmen escorted the handcuffed gangster through the station parking lot, and as they placed him into the automobile, his allies struck.

The deafening roar of machine-gun fire ripped through the peaceful morning. Five men were killed: two officers, a federal agent, and a Kansas City police chief. The fifth was Frank Nash, accidentally killed by the bullets from his allies' guns.

According to Becky, apparitions are seen throughout the Union Station. She mentioned a peculiar sighting in the Union Station Historical Room. It was after hours and the room was off-limits to the public, so when a member of the security team glanced at the monitor and saw a figure on a bench there, he sent a guard to investigate.

When the guard radioed dispatch, he reported that, "There is no one here."

"Yes, there is," the dispatcher insisted, "I can see them through the monitor."

Though the man appeared on the monitor, he was not visible to the guard. And then, as the dispatcher scrutinized the screen, he could not believe what he was seeing. The figure on the bench did not have a head.

"We think it may have been the ghost of Frank Nash," said Becky, explaining that the gangster's head was nearly severed by machine-gun bullets.

KANSAS CITY UNION STATION
30 W. Pershing Road
Kansas City, Missouri 64108
www.unionstation.com

NOT THERE

When it comes to seeing ghosts in the mirror, it is not always straightforward. What does it mean when the apparitions have no reflections?

Paula Brown from Dallas, Texas, wrote to me about her odd encounter.

I was standing in line at the ticket counter in Dallas-Fort Worth International Airport. It was just post 9/11. I noticed a young couple ahead of me. They were standing side by side, holding hands. They were both quite tall. I am five foot seven, yet they both towered over me. The woman had long blond hair and the man, too, was blond. They looked special, even from behind. They were somehow extraordinarily attractive. They were dressed casually in modern attire. I think that one or both of them had on tan, khaki, safari-type gear. I don't remember them speaking to each other.

I realized there was a convex mirror overhead and I wanted to see their faces. I glanced up at the mirror, and I could see myself, but I could not see the couple's reflection. I found myself thinking vampires!

It was an intriguing scenario. Not long after I received Paula's letter, I spoke with her.

She told me how she had walked around, standing in various spots, trying to position herself so she could see the couple's reflection in the security mirror. But only the empty floor appeared in the space that should have mirrored the beautiful people.

"I was really startled," she confided. "I could not make sense of it."

The enigma continued for several minutes. When the line started moving, Paula momentarily forgot the phenomenon and became preoccupied with finding her ticket and identification and suddenly, it was her turn at the ticket counter.

When she was settled on the plane, she again wondered about the mysterious couple. "It occurred to me that I should have noticed them at the ticket counter," she said. But they had seemingly vanished. In retrospect, another thing struck her as strange: The people were almost unnaturally still.

Though a few years have passed since the perplexing encounter, Paula often finds her thoughts drifting back to that day. *Vampires? Angels? Ghosts?*

She will never know who the people really were.

Ghost Station

A pale child skips over the polished floors. The apparitions of drowned victims float through the basement. A passenger from a bygone time waits for a phantom train.

These are just a few of the ghosts haunting Denver's Union Station, according to Kevin Rucker, historian and director of LoDo Historic Walking Tours.

Kevin and his wife, Darcey, regularly lead tours through the Mile High City and are familiar with both its history and its haunting. The couple has collected enough firsthand accounts of ghost sightings to recognize Union Station as one of the spookiest places in town. "Sometimes a soldier in a World War II uniform is seen pacing outside the terminal, awaiting a train," Kevin said.

Not everyone survived when the 1933 flood filled the station's basement. "Six workmen drowned in the basement and they are sometimes seen," he said.

The victim of an 1800s tragedy still roams the Denver Union Station. (Leslie Rule)

It is not the ghosts of the workmen, however, that terrify the security guards who patrol the station. Instead, they are so frightened by a little girl that, "they refuse to walk inside the lobby after midnight."

It is then, Kevin explained, that a small girl skips along the second-floor balcony.

The child may not know she is dead, though she left her earthly body over a century ago. According to Kevin, the eight-year-old lost her life in a horrible freak accident in 1894. She was standing beneath an enormous chandelier when it crashed down upon her.

Denver Union Station
Wynkoop and Seventeenth Street
Denver, Colorado 80219

Lower Downtown (LoDo) Historic Walking Tours
www.lodo.org

Though folks usually check into hotels, motels, and bed and breakfasts with plans to sleep through the night, when they stay in the following spots they may find themselves red eyed and yawning in the morning light—unless they request a *nonhaunted room*.

Even the most haunted hotels in the world have their share of quiet suites. Yet more and more people are requesting haunted rooms, happily trading in restful nights for *restless* nights so that they might experience the thrill of a spirit encounter.

The following places are recommended to ghost enthusiasts in search of active sites.

THE HAUNTED
SEELBACH HOTEL

Missi Nussbaum took a job at the Seelbach Hotel because she was bored. It was summertime 1992, and she was looking forward to her wedding day in the upcoming fall. But she had time on her hands so she applied for a job as a maid at the historic hotel in downtown Louisville, Kentucky. She loved the rich elegance of the place. "I thought it would be fun to work in the building," she told me.

The beauty of the hotel and the palpable sense of history beckoned her and soon Missi was employed there. It was routine work, vacuuming and scrubbing and changing sheets—until the day she was sent to the tenth floor by herself. Ballrooms and meeting areas dominate the tenth floor, with fewer rooms available for overnight guests, she explained. "The top-floor rooms were rarely booked. I had been sent up to do some freshening up before a big party arrived. Typically, room keepers work in pairs, but I was by myself that day. I was straightening the beds, spraying air freshener, and dusting."

Ever the multitasker, Missi decided to catch up on her favorite soap operas so she turned on the television and watched while she worked. "My supervisor caught me," she admitted. When the woman admonished her, Missi sheepishly assured her that she would keep the television turned off.

"I was on edge after that," she told me. "I kept expecting my supervisor to sneak up on me and catch me doing something wrong. It felt like someone was watching me."

It was an uneasy feeling and though Missi tried to focus on plumping pillows and polishing furniture, she could not shake the niggling sense of eyes upon her. The sensation continued as she worked in a corner room with a unique configuration. "In most of the rooms, the mirror hangs next to the door, but in the corner room the mirror is placed opposite the doorway," she explained.

As she bent to straighten a wrinkle in the bedspread, the inkling that she was being watched intensified. She glanced up at the mirror and saw a woman. She appeared to be standing in the doorway directly behind her, though Missi's own body blocked most of the image. "All I could see was her head," she said. In that instant, she took in the pale complexion, light hair, and bland expression. "There was no malice, yet the room became freezing cold and I got an awful feeling."

Missi turned to the doorway, expecting to see a woman standing there.

No one was there!

"I looked back at the mirror and she was *still* in the mirror doorway!"

Missi ran. "I could not get out of there fast enough. My skin was crawling!"

Years later, she still shivers when she talks about it. "It was weird because I'd always thought I'd be fascinated if I ever saw a ghost," she said. "But there was a physical sensation of having suddenly taken sick. It was dreadful. I did not go back up there that day. They had to get someone else to finish the rooms."

Though Missi was not aware of it at the time, she was not the first or the *last* to encounter a ghost at the Seelbach Hotel.

❧

Brothers Otto and Louis Seelbach celebrated the grand opening of their hotel on May 1, 1905, as a crowd of 25,000 people gathered. Inspired by French Renaissance architecture, the ten-story stone and brick structure was the tallest building in Louisville and the first fire-proof hotel in the city, according to Larry Johnson, longtime Seelbach bell captain and author of *The Seelbach: A Centennial Salute to Louis-ville's Grand Hotel*.

Larry knows the hotel inside and out, and can tell guests that the marbled walls were imported from Europe, that nine United States presidents have stayed there, and that F. Scott Fitzgerald was kicked out of the luxury hotel in 1918 after drinking too much bourbon. (Fitzgerald later used the Seelbach as the setting for the wedding of Tom and Daisy in his acclaimed 1925 novel, *The Great Gatsby*.)

In his three decades at the hotel, Larry has become aware of the ghosts. Though he and Missi Nussbaum have never spoken about her spirit encounter, the historian has talked with other employees who saw apparitions materialize in the hotel mirrors.

In December of 1983 an employee was alone in the hotel's first-floor Otto Café when he had a startling experience. It was after midnight, according to Larry, and the young man was busy cleaning the tables when he glanced up at the large mirror on the south wall. He saw an elderly lady and assumed she was homeless. She wore tattered clothing and a floppy, orange hat. He felt a twinge of pity and decided to let her warm up a little before sending her back out into the frosty winter night.

As he busied himself cleaning, he casually noticed that the woman had made no move to leave. When it was time to ask her to go, he turned to speak to her but found himself alone. He turned back to see that the mirror image remained.

Thoroughly shaken and unsure what else to do, he called security who soon discovered something strange. According to their records, exactly one year before, another employee had reported an identical sighting.

Larry is especially intrigued by another ghost at the Seelbach, known as the "Lady in Blue." The dark-haired woman in a blue dress has been seen on several occasions, always walking into the elevator. A woman boarding an elevator is not that unusual, *unless* the doors are shut as she enters. The Lady in Blue steps right *through* the closed elevator doors.

Who is she and why does she haunt the elevator?

Larry mentions the Seelbach's ghosts in his book and also includes information from a newspaper clipping about a 1936 tragedy that occurred at the hotel.

Patricia Wilson was found atop the service elevator. By the time she was discovered, she had been dead for several hours. According to the account, the twenty-four-year-old woman had been planning a reunion with her estranged husband but *he* had been killed just days earlier in a car accident.

Since the 1992 discovery of the old newspaper story, people have speculated that Patricia Wilson committed suicide because of her husband's death, or was so distraught with grief that she was simply not paying attention and carelessly stepped into the empty elevator shaft.

I, however, have found something that indicates Patricia's death may be the result of something far more sinister. After many hours of searching archives, I put my hands on an article that sent a chill skipping down the back of my neck. If the implications from the old newspaper are true, Patricia did not commit suicide. Nor did she have an accident.

Patricia Wilson may have been murdered.

Finding all of the answers to the fatal elevator mystery is as challenging as putting together a jigsaw puzzle with pieces lost beneath the sofa cushions. Eyewitnesses have passed away, old records have been shredded, and only bits of the story remain in the form of neatly printed newspaper columns with scant details.

When the young woman's broken body was discovered on top of a linen elevator at the Seelbach Hotel on July 15, 1936, police were quoted in the newspapers, saying that she had been "a party girl." It was a dismissive label to slap on someone who had just been killed. And it invited a "blame the victim" mentality.

Patricia was supposedly at a "drinking party" at the hotel just prior to her disappearance. She had been missing for hours before the discovery of her lifeless body. A young woman with a troubled marriage who attended drinking parties did not garner much respect in the 1930s.

Murder, *however*, is serious. And one would think that even the murder of a "party girl" would warrant some scrutiny. If they suspected foul play, surely the police would investigate.

Maybe not.

Crime had previously gone unpunished at the Seelbach. The hotel's own Web site boasts that gangsters were welcomed there. Celebrity gangster Al Capone played cards there, and, in fact, had a special mirror sent from Chicago and installed so that he could "watch his back." In addition, he had access to secret passageways and a tunnel beneath the hotel so that he could hide from police.

The Seelbach Web site also notes that the hotel was "the center of Kentucky's bourbon and whiskey country" during prohibition in the 1920s.

Al Capone was in prison at the time of Patricia Wilson's death. So he, of course, was not her killer. But the notorious gangster was not the only unsavory character to swagger through Louisville.

How much power would a man have to brandish in order to escape prosecution for the homicide of a young woman? What if he was a former prosecuting attorney, a general, a governor, *and* a publisher of a Kentucky newspaper?

It would be a year before just such a man was accused of beating Patricia and throwing her down the elevator shaft. It was not a criminal charge, however, but a civil suit, that fingered him as an ice blooded killer.

When General Henry H. Denhardt learned of the suit against him, he dismissed it as "absurd and ridiculous." In a brief July 6, 1937, newspaper article the sixty-year-old divorced Bowling Green, Kentucky, politician said, "I never heard of that girl. I was not in the hotel at that time."

General Denhardt scoffed at the $70,000 lawsuit leveled at him by Edward C. Langan, Jefferson County public administrator. The suit alleged that the six-foot two, 230-pound "Denhardt had assaulted, beat, and bruised Miss Wilson, causing her to fall down the elevator shaft."

The general soon retaliated by suing *Langan* for over double the amount for damages caused by the suit against him. He claimed his enemies were trying to destroy him, and that the suit was "deliberate and maliciously filed" to harm him and rob him of his precious military rank.

The articles about Patricia Wilson's mysterious death were not much more than footnotes to front-page stories of Henry Denhardt's bigger troubles. For fifteen short weeks after Patricia's death, a bullet from his .45 revolver killed another Kentucky woman.

Mrs. Verna Garr Taylor was a forty-three-year-old widow and the mother of two teenaged daughters. The newspapers heralded her as a slender, dark-eyed beauty of high society. She owned a successful laundry business near her home in La Grange, Kentucky, and moved in the same social circles as the general. He was smitten with her and they were engaged to be married.

What did Verna Garr Taylor see in Henry Denhardt? He was nearly twenty years her senior. The papers described him as portly and bald.

But Henry Denhardt had an impressive résumé. He had served in three wars, been the governor of Kentucky, held the rank of brigadier general in the Kentucky National Guard, and lieutenant colonel in the army. He had been prosecuting attorney of Bowling Green for ten years and had also served two terms as county judge of Warren County. On top of all that, he had partnered with his brother as publisher of the *Bowling Green Times Journal*.

Maybe Verna was drawn to his status, wealth, and power. Or perhaps she really loved him. It didn't matter. She was dead in a ditch before they could be married.

On November 6, 1936, Verna and Henry went for a drive. As they headed along a lonely country road the car stalled. Verna walked to a nearby gas station to get help. Oddly, Henry was quiet and sullen and remained seated in the car as Good Samaritans pushed it. Verna made excuses for him, saying he was sick.

Gunshots were heard within an hour, and Verna was found dead near the broken-down car. She had been killed by the general's service revolver. Henry claimed that they had taken a drive to alleviate Verna's headache and that she was distraught because her teenage daughter was opposed to their upcoming marriage. Verna, he insisted, had suggested a suicide pact. (Later, however, he would testify that she was upset about his rival, a handsome twenty-six-year-old laundry truck driver, Chester Woolfolk. Chester and Verna had feelings for each other, and Henry suggested that Verna was suicidal because she was unhappy about the fact that Chester was pursuing her.)

Verna's three brothers were grief stricken and outraged. Roy Garr, Jack Garr, and veterinarian Dr. E. S. Garr urged the prosecutor to press charges. In April 1937, the general went on trial for Verna's murder.

The State said that the general had killed her because she had rejected him. The two-week murder trial ended on May 6, 1937. The jury of eleven farmers and a filling-station attendant deadlocked with seven voting for his acquittal.

"It's a great vindication," the general crowed to reporters, though he was well aware that a second trial would be scheduled.

On September 20, 1937, the eve of General Denhardt's new trial, he met with his three attorneys in his room at the Armstrong Hotel in Shelbyville. Around 10:00 p.m. the general and his attorney, Rode Myers, went out for beers. As they walked back to the Armstrong, they saw the Garr brothers. The three men got out of a parked automobile and strode deliberately toward the startled general who took one look at their set faces and ran toward the entrance of the hotel. He fumbled frantically for the knob, and when the door would not budge, he threw his bulk against it.

Two of the Garr brothers drew their guns and seven bullets entered the big man's head and chest. Henry Denhardt rolled into the hotel doorway and died.

The brothers turned themselves into the police, claiming that they had fired at the general in self-defense, though no weapon was found on him.

Charges were filed against the brothers and the courtroom was filled with spectators who cheered for them. Public sentiment was with the men who had avenged their sister's murder.

Soon Roy and Jack were acquitted. Dr. Garr, shell-shocked from the war, was sent to a mental hospital for observation for a short time before all charges were dropped.

With two women and their suspected killer dead, the truth is as elusive as a piano note in a breeze. Yet some odd "coincidences" remain.

Within a fifteen-week period, three people with connections to Henry Denhardt died in "accidents." According to the lawsuit filed on behalf of Patricia Wilson's estate, the general had some sort of a relationship with her—a relationship that was so emotionally charged it ended with her murder in the elevator shaft.

If indeed, Patricia *was* romantically involved with Henry, it is suspect that both she and her husband should die violently just when they were about to reconcile and leave Henry out in the cold.

If Patricia did indeed have a connection to Henry as the lawsuit had alleged, what was the nature of the relationship? Were they dating? If so, was he enraged to learn she was going back to her husband?

General Denhardt's detractors claimed that he had plenty of henchmen to do his dirty work, some suggesting that he had an accomplice in Verna's murder. Perhaps one of these helpers had staged Patricia's husband's car accident.

Many killers in recent years have been successfully prosecuted after staging car accidents to cover up homicides, but forensics in the 1930s was far less sophisticated than it is today and myriad guilty people literally got away with murder.

In the 1930s, "a good old boys' club" ruled the underbelly of the Seelbach. Patricia Wilson was probably not their only victim. In the halcyon days of his romance with Verna, the bold Henry Denhardt likely returned to the scene of the crime to show off his new fiancée and to dine in the elegant Seelbach restaurant.

After her violent death, Verna's restless soul may have been drawn to the tragic hotel to commiserate with Patricia. For all we know, Henry is there too.

SEELBACH HILTON LOUISVILLE
500 Fourth Street
Louisville, Kentucky 40202
(502) 585-3200
www.seelbachhilton.com

THORNEWOOD CASTLE

When it comes to haunted places, it is hard to say if one is more haunted then another. Some may *seem* more haunted simply because more paranormal investigators have visited there and collected more data. Other places may have been covered so extensively in the media that more folks come forward to share their spirit encounters, and the ghostly reputation grows.

I have never stopped to count how many haunted locations I have been to. After researching four books on ghosts, my files are thick. Yet, of all the places I've seen, it is one in my own backyard that gets my vote for the spookiest *and* the most beautiful.

Thornewood Castle in Lakewood, Washington, is an exquisite, three-story mansion with English-style gardens and a view of American Lake.

Chester Thorne, one of the founders of the Port of Tacoma, built the castle for his wife Anna and their family. He strived for authenticity and imported materials from a real European castle. Three ships were commissioned to deliver the recycled brick, oak paneling, magnificent oak staircase, and medieval stained glass. After three years of construction, the castle was completed in 1911.

ABC cast the mansion for Stephen King's miniseries *Rose Red*, choosing it over dozens of other places throughout America and Canada. In an eerie "coincidence," the appearance of Thornewood Castle closely matched the "house with feelings" that sprung from the horror writer's imagination. The castle starred as the very haunted mansion in the movie, airing for the first time in 2002.

The castle was briefly mentioned in my book *Ghosts Among Us* and now, four years later, the ghosts are still active. I've spent the night in Thornewood Castle twice in the last couple of years, and each time, I experienced something odd.

The many mirrors of Thornewood Castle may be the key to the haunting. (Leslie Rule)

What lurks in the hallway of this sumptuous bed and breakfast? (Leslie Rule)

The first time I stayed there was the night before my friend's wedding and we had the mansion to ourselves. She and I stayed up late and practiced for the upcoming ceremony, in our pajamas and stocking feet, on the shiny hardwood floor of the enormous living room.

The next morning the manager asked us if we had unscrewed the lightbulbs in the two fixtures in the living room. We had not. The fixtures were high on the wall, and we would have needed a ladder to reach them. If it had been just one loosened lightbulb, we could have shrugged it off. But *two*?

During my second overnight visit, my friend and I once again had the place to ourselves. It was about 2:00 a.m. and I was on the second floor taking photos of the hallway when I sensed someone behind me. The feeling was so strong that it did not occur to me that a being without a body was watching me. I turned around but there was no one there. My friend was in our room, four doors down.

Dozens of people had described that very sensation to me, but for the first time, I *knew* what it felt like. And I was spooked. This occurred outside the room named for former resident and present ghost, Anna Thorne.

A smiling apparition has been witnessed in "Anna's room." As brides admire themselves in Anna's century-old mirror, they have been startled to see the reflection of an older lady sitting on the window seat. Perhaps it was Anna who watched me in the hall.

Later, I was awakened from a sound sleep to find my bed shaking. No earthquake was reported in our area, and there was no reason for the trembling. I surmised that phantom hands had shaken the bed in an effort to rattle me—*literally*.

Others have had more profound experiences there. An employee told me of the bride-to-be and her mother who stayed in Anna's room. They awoke in the night to the sounds of music, laughter, and chatter coming from downstairs. It sounded like a festive event with many people. So they got up and dressed, excited about joining the impromptu party.

As the two women ventured down the wide, graceful staircase, silence swallowed the sound and suddenly all was still. They tiptoed down the steps and their mouths fell open. The vast room was empty. They hurried back to bed, shivering with the mystery and eager for morning to come.

On another occasion, an employee was polishing the crystal in the dining room when she heard a child's giggle. "It sounded like a little boy, running and playing," she told me, and then described how she had turned around to find no one there.

Had one of the owner's grandchildren raced into the room and out again?

Though she knew that no one could move that fast, she searched for a child anyway, just to be sure. "I found the owner sitting in another room," she said. "No one was visiting. We were alone there."

"Maybe the child was outside," I suggested, grasping for a logical explanation.

She shook her head and explained that the laughter was directly behind her, not more than a few feet away.

I asked her if she were ever afraid.

"No. I've worked here a long time," she said. But I thought I saw fear dart through her brown eyes. She pointed at the ceiling. There, distinct against the white ceiling, was perhaps the strangest thing of all. A single, small dirty footprint. It was the unmistakable mark of a child's bare foot. The ornate ceiling is about twenty feet high, and there is no reason for the footprint to be there.

Another employee had an encounter that left him shaking. He heard someone in the kitchen as he worked in an adjacent room. He figured that either a fellow employee or the owner was in there, so he decided to duck in and say hello.

He grabbed the doorknob and twisted, but the door would not budge. It was as if someone were pressing against the door from the inside. Why in the world would someone bar his entrance?

He decided it was an intruder, and ran outside just as a manager drove up. "Someone is in the kitchen!" he cried. "They won't let me in."

When the manager tried the door, it opened easily. They looked around and found no sign that anyone had been there.

The ghosts who inhabit Thornewood Castle may remain for a variety of reasons. Some may be past residents, some may have arrived by ship with the recycled castle materials, and some may have come in with the many antiques purchased by the owners. Perhaps some have come through the mirrors.

It was with a shrewd eye that I counted the mirrors in the mansion. I stopped counting at one hundred. If indeed, mirrors are passageways for ghosts, Thornewood Castle has no shortage of portals—and no shortage of ghosts.

THORNEWOOD CASTLE
8601 N. Thorne Lane SW
Lakewood, Washington 98498
(253) 584-4393
www.thornewoodcastle.com

Thornewood Castle and its grounds are inaccessible to those without reservations. Check the Web site for information on special events open to the public.

We Hear You Knocking . . .

Though eerie moans and rattling chains are favorite ghostly sound effects for Halloween and may be prevalent in Europe's haunted castles, these noises are heard less often in America's haunted places. The most commonly reported unexplained sounds associated with ghosts in the United States are:

1. **Footsteps**

   The phenomenon of phantom footsteps is frequently found in haunted spots. The footsteps often clomp up or down stairs, or tread through hallways in a set path that follows a recurring pattern. Residents of haunted houses with carpeted floors sometimes report that it sounds as if feet are walking over bare floors.

2. **Doors opening and shutting**

   The sound of a door opening or closing may be included in the pattern of the disembodied footsteps mentioned above, but can also occur on its own.

3. **Knocking**

   Enigmatic raps or knocks on walls and doors are often heard by folks who live in or visit haunted spots.

4. **Voices**

   It is common for people in paranormally active places to hear disembodied voices, sometimes several that seem to be engaged in conversation. Very frequently, a voice will call the name of the witness and can often sound like an individual who could logically be there, but is *not*. New employees at haunted places such as restaurants and hotels often report this phenomenon on their very first day. It is almost as if the ghost is initiating them.

5. **Throat clearing**

   The sound of coughing or a clearing of the throat is another noise associated with ghosts.

6. **Crying**

   The sound of women, children, or babies crying is also noted at many haunted places. The weeping may sound faint and faraway, or as loud as if it is in the next room, emanating through a thin wall.

7. **Ringing phone or doorbell**

   The ghostly rings of telephones and doorbells (sometimes nonexistent) have often been reported in active spots.

8. **Music**

   It may be a few stray notes from the piano or an entire concert. Ghostly tunes play for startled witnesses in many haunted places. Most often, the music is heard from another room, and people assume a live person is responsible. If they go to investigate, the music abruptly stops as they near the suspected source.

9. **Screams**

   The unsettling sound of a sudden scream can wake people in the night at haunted places, although they have been heard at all times of the day and night. While disembodied screams have indeed been reported, they are more common in movies about haunted houses than in actual haunted houses.

Six Scents

Inexplicable scents are among the most reported phenomena associated with spirit visits and haunted places. While some are pleasant fragrances, others are repulsive odors.

Here are the most common smells reported in haunted places:

1. **Cigars and pipes**

   The phantom aroma of cigar or pipe smoke is frequently linked to ghostly activity. In cases where the identity of the ghost is known, the distinctive fragrance of the brand of tobacco can often be matched to the entity in question.

2. Perfume

Perfume—particularly of a flowery nature—also tops the list of commonly noted spirit scents. Often people will recognize the perfume of a departed loved one while sensing their spirit near, and take great comfort from the experience.

Many curators of historic homes turned museum have credited the mystifying fragrance to the ghosts of long-ago ladies who once resided there.

3. Cigarettes

Though not as commonly reported as the scent of cigars and pipes, cigarettes are also smelled in places where the deceased once smoked, despite the fact the structure has had years to air out. The smell materializes suddenly and can just as suddenly disappear.

4. Cooking food

It is not unusual to note the smell of cooking food wafting through haunted places, usually in the kitchen. Folks often find their appetites piqued only to be disappointed when they encounter a cold, empty stove.

5. Sulfur

The less pleasant odor of sulfur is lower down on the list, yet still noted in many haunted spots. This scent can be associated with a less than peaceful haunting.

6. Rotting flesh

In places bordering on disturbing, the horrid stench of rotting flesh is occasionally noted. This frightening assault to the senses can be enough to send residents packing. Research will sometimes reveal that a violent death, such as a murder, took place on the premises, sometimes centuries before.

SOMETHING IN THE WATER

The two middle-aged ladies giggled as Keith Winge walked by. He turned to smile at the women, who were huddled in the hallway of the second floor of the Elms Resort in Excelsior Springs, Missouri.

"What's so funny?" he asked politely.

"Nothing," one said. "We're just waiting to see the little girl."

"Oh." He knew who they meant. "Enjoy your stay," he said as he headed back to his office where he served as the resort's director of sales and marketing. *Word gets around fast,* he thought. For it was just a couple of weeks earlier that ten-year-olds on a field trip had stood in the very hallway and seen the now-infamous girl. The entire class of fifth graders had claimed that they had seen the ghostly child race right past them and disappear into the wall.

✦

For some, it was the last hope. Pain shot through their withered limbs. Or breathing was labored as heartbeats grew faint. A few had headaches so bad that they weren't sure they wanted to live another day.

Go to Excelsior Springs, they were told. It will help. The water can heal you! It helped my uncle Bert. We thought he was a goner, but he's still kicking.

Maybe just believing that the water would help made it so. For many came away from the springs feeling invigorated and hopeful.

It all began in 1880 when farmer Travis Mellion saw his daughter healed of her skin disease after bathing in and drinking the rust-colored water that some called "pizen" (poison) because of its brownish appearance.

Word spread about the child's recovery and within a year, the town overflowed with visitors who sought cures in the healing mineral waters. An industry was born. Factories bottled water and ginger ale there, and bathhouses were plentiful. Hotels were erected, and the good ones featured private baths and "hydrotherapy."

The Elms Hotel was built to cater to the wealthy who came to town for the healing spring water. It opened in 1888 and burned down ten years later. The new Elms Hotel was built in 1908 and burned down a year later.

The third time was the charm for the new hotel. It was built in 1912, only a short distance from the original structure and thanks to a steel skeleton and a facade of native stone, it still stands today. The Elms Resort and Spa, now owned by the city of Excelsior Springs, is a charming, historical building surrounded by lightly forested acreage.

Excelsior Springs was once a booming town. A depot near the Elms saw droves of people arrive by train, and the streets bustled with

The sick and dying once hoped that the magical waters of the Elms Resort would heal them. (Leslie Rule)

Do unseen entities rock in these chairs outside of the historic Elms Resort? (Leslie Rule)

tourists. During the 1930s, gangster Al Capone was a regular at the hotel, where he had his own special quarters with a window facing the front so that he could watch for the police.

In the 1960s, however, business in Excelsior Springs went downhill after a national magazine published a story discrediting claims that the water had special healing powers.

No one knows who may be hiding behind the trees on the grounds of the Elms Resort. (Leslie Rule)

The Elms Resort suffered along with the rest of the enterprises in town. It served a stint as a veteran's hospital and afterward sat abandoned for years. The neighborhood kids turned it into their private playground, climbing through the broken windows for a game of hide-and-seek in the dark, dusty halls. One of those kids, now grown and living a few doors down from the hotel, told me that his sister had encountered a glowing apparition in the dilapidated building. It was the ghost of a maid, pushing a cleaning cart through the shadows.

The refurbishing apparently did not scare away the stubborn spirits for both employees and guests continue to see them. Waitress Cathy Zeller told me that the chandelier in the ballroom sometimes begins to sway, as if unseen children are swinging from it. And she once saw a ball of light zip through the ballroom.

With so many critically ill people seeking out healing waters at the hotel, surely a few must have died. I've searched, but have yet to find a case of a little girl dying on the premises. The story behind the ghost child in the second floor hall remains a mystery.

I did, however, find that James Albertus Tawney died at age sixty-four at the Elms on June 13, 1919. He was a former Minnesota congressman and sought treatment at the Elms for heart trouble. Though we usually find that paranormally active sites are tied to more violent or tragic deaths, we cannot rule out

Jay Fanning poses near the spot where he encountered an unusual apparition. (Leslie Rule)

the possibility that the congressman still walks the premises. If he does, he is not alone.

A number of ghosts are believed to haunt the Elms. Keith Winge told me that he had heard that an Elvis impersonator committed suicide in the hotel, though he did not know any details. Some say they have seen his ghost.

While the hotel has a heated outside pool and hot tubs, it also has an indoor pool in the basement of the building. Jay Fanning, the nighttime maintenance man, took me there and pointed out the spot where he had seen an unusual apparition late one night. In the fleeting moment he glimpsed the ghost, he thought the fellow was dressed like a mime, with dark clothing and a painted white face. He sat in a deckchair beside the pool and stared at Jay intently before vanishing. "He looked as real and solid as any person," he told me.

Jay was not aware of the suicidal Elvis impersonator, and it is possible that the ghost belonged to him. The dark clothing and the white made-up face could easily have been part of an Elvis costume.

The lanes of the lap pool form a loop, like a track designed for joggers. Old-timers in town told me that the pool was once used to exercise racehorses. The trainers, they said, would stand outside the pool and lead the swimming horses.

Whatever else took place down there was probably not always positive. For the basement pool has a creepy feel to it. It is not surprising that so many people are afraid to swim alone there.

THE ELMS RESORT AND SPA
401 Regent Street
Excelsior Springs, Missouri 64024
1-800-THE ELMS
www.elmsresort.com

THE OXFORD HOTEL

"I think the Oxford is more haunted than the Stanley Hotel. There is an eeriness about it. It has the same feel as the Myrtles."

That is what Janice Oberding had to say when I asked her to recollect our stay at the Denver, Colorado, historic hotel. Janice, the author of six nonfiction books of ghost stories from the California and Nevada area, joined me and our mutual friend, paranormal investigator Debby Constantino, for two days of research at the Oxford Hotel in early November 2006.

Ghost aficionados will be impressed to hear that Janice named the Oxford in the same breath as the Myrtles and the Stanley Hotel. Famously haunted, each has gained national attention.

The Myrtles, a bed and breakfast in St. Francisville, Louisiana, is promoted as home to a number of ghosts, most notably a slave who was allegedly hanged after she baked deadly oleander in a birthday cake that killed several people.

Denver's Oxford Hotel may be the city's most haunted. (Leslie Rule)

Staff at the Stanley Hotel in Estes Park, Colorado, boast that it is so haunted that it inspired Stephen King to pen his blockbuster novel *The Shining*.

If the Oxford Hotel ranks with these highly haunted locations, it is surprising that it has gotten so little national attention. But Janice will get no argument from me. I've been to all three places, and the Oxford is definitely up there on the creepy scale.

When I made arrangements for our stay, I e-mailed a manager and requested the hotel's most haunted room. She quickly responded, securing reservations for us in room 320. She did not, however, offer details of the room's haunting *or* its history.

That was fine with me, for as a writer I often like to experience a place raw. My impressions will be baked and served soon enough. Our trio checked into the Oxford with open minds.

The five-story brick hotel struck me as lovely and quaint. When it first opened its doors in 1891, visitors certainly did not think of it as "quaint." Most of them had never seen such modern conveniences. Guests not only enjoyed the luxury of electric lights and heated rooms, they no longer had to climb the stairs. The amazed folks boarded an elevator, dubbed the "vertical railway," and marveled at the invention as they rode to the brick building's fifth floor.

By today's standards, the Oxford is clean and comfortable with a charming ambience. Soon after we checked in, Janice, Debby, and I took a stroll. As we reached Wynkoop Street, Debby suddenly said, "It feels like there are tunnels under this street." Though it was her first time in Denver and she knew little about the Mile High City, she had just zeroed in on something significant.

While researching archives the following day, I learned that though historians have yet to verify it, they have long suspected that a secret tunnel did indeed travel beneath Wynkoop Street connecting the Union Station to the Oxford so that important guests could discreetly arrive at the hotel.

Though she is shy about presenting herself as psychic, Debby has a keen sixth sense. This may be why she is so successful in recording phantom voices, an endeavor that seems to reap more impressive results when a sensitive is present.

Readers of *When the Ghost Screams: True Stories of Victims Who Haunt* will remember that I introduced Mark and Debby Constantino in the case of the earthbound spirits of the Donner Party in Truckee, California. Our group recorded what we believe to be the ghostly voices of pioneers who starved to death when they were snowbound in the spot in the mid-nineteenth century.

The Constantinos are a husband and wife team who are experts in the art of gathering Electronic Voice Phenomena (EVP). Mark could not join us for our stay in Denver, but Debby was eager to begin recording there.

While Debby and Janice were excited about researching the haunted Oxford, they were also afraid. Neither would spend one minute alone in our room.

The suite consisted of two adjoining rooms. I slept in the back room, and Debby and Janice shared the front room. One day as I snoozed, the two went out for a while and when they returned they slipped the key into the lock and were startled by the sound of retreating footsteps.

"That night I slept on the cot," Debby recalled. "Janice was on the couch. I clearly heard two men talking, but I could not make out what they said," she remembered, explaining that the disembodied voices seemed to come from two invisible men sitting on the couch. "It freaked me out!" She shuddered with the memory of the eerie mumbling.

"A bit later that night, I felt something lightly touch me across my stomach," said Debby. "At that point I asked Janice if she would sleep on the cot with me."

The spooked pair stuck together, and I explored by myself through much of our stay. My time was dominated by photographing haunted locations and searching library archives, while they concentrated on investigating the Oxford.

Janice and Debby roamed the Oxford at all hours of the day and night. They carried tape recorders and captured many phantom voices. After they learned that the basement men's room was particularly haunted, they slipped downstairs where the lower floor was closed off to the public and entered the large tiled room. Apparently the ghost did not appreciate the ladies' intrusion in the men's room for Debby taped an angry male voice, snarling, "Get the (expletive) out."

Around midnight of our second night, the two were standing at the top of the stairs, above the bell desk, when a shadowy figure darted past them.

Many guests and employees have had ghost encounters at the Oxford. A manager told me about a cleaning crew who reported to her immediately after an unsettling experience. They regularly cleaned the annexed addition to the Oxford, where rooms are now used as offices. "As they approached the door to an office, a woman in a white dress floated *through* the closed door," the manager said, adding that the crew was visibly shaken.

I contacted historian Kevin Rucker of LoDo Historic Walking Tours to ask for his impressions about the haunted Oxford. In addition to interviewing folks about their ghost encounters, Kevin is well acquainted with the archives of the Denver Public Library where he does much of his research. According to Kevin, a number of restless spirits wander the hotel, sometimes materializing in the mirrors.

As guests wash up in the downstairs men's room, they have glanced into the mirror and seen the reflection of a cowboy. The vestige of the Old West paces behind the witnesses, but when they turn around they see that they are alone.

Kevin also shared the account of the dancing teenager who employees have glimpsed in the mirror in the ballroom. "She looks to be about fourteen and is pirouetting," he said.

On another occasion, he told me, the hotel suffered a power outage in the night. A guest staying in a room on the third floor got up to use the bathroom, holding a penlight to find her way. She pointed the thin stream of light into the bathroom and was shocked to see a child perched on the toilet, solemnly gazing up at her. "The girl was about seven years old and wore a lace nightgown," said the historian.

According to Kevin, Bat Masterson lived in room 320 in the 1890s. "He killed a man there," he said, adding that single men rarely manage to spend an entire night in the room. "If a single man checks into room 320 he will show up downstairs at the front desk in the middle of the night, claiming someone is in his room. Single females and couples have no problems."

There is another account circulating about room 320, though Kevin did not refer to it. The story goes that a man caught his wife with another man and shot them both dead in the third floor suite at the Oxford. As a result, room 320 has been dubbed, the "Murder Room."

While all of the above may have indeed taken place in the hotel, I have yet to find documentation to verify the information. I did, however, find something that may be the key to the most impressive EVP that Debby Constantino obtained at the Oxford.

It is a female voice, speaking so distinctly that there is no mistaking the words for static. "It is a class A recording," said Debby of the voice she captured in the hallway outside of room 320.

The woman's words are clear and her message is chilling. "I'm sick."
"I'm sick."

Sick or sick in the head?

That was the question I asked myself when I read a startling account. For after many fruitless trips to the archives, I was finally rewarded with a two-inch column of blocky words, printed over a century ago in the *New York Times*.

On Friday, September 9, 1898, a distraught young woman pointed a gun at her lover and pulled the trigger. She then turned the gun on herself. A bullet pierced her broken heart and she died instantly in the hotel room.

They had checked into the Oxford, registering themselves as husband and wife and giving their names as H. Rockwell from Greeley, Colorado, and Florence Montague from Pittsburgh. The names were aliases. Rockwell was actually W. H. Lawrence, and while he *was* married, his female companion was not his wife. She was later identified as Florence Richardson. She was about twenty-four, and he was forty-five.

The man died in St. Luke's Hospital on the Sunday after the shooting. He had a family in Cleveland, Ohio, and owned an interest in Ohio Farmer Publishing, where his brother was president. His brother came from Cleveland to retrieve his remains.

Several brief newspaper pieces told the story. Florence had lived at the Oxford for several weeks and had been planning "an overland trip by wagon" with her "husband." One account described her as a woman "of dissolute character."

Paranormal researchers note a strong correlation between traumatic death and haunted locations. The emotion and violence associated with Florence's demise definitely make her a strong candidate for an Oxford ghost. She may be the ghost who spoke to Debby's recorder. *"I'm sick."*

If only we could hear the whole story that eight inches of fading newspaper print cannot tell. Did Florence want more than her lover could give her? Did she know he was married? Had she just learned the truth? Was he leaving her? Was she with child and suffering morning sickness?

Is Florence's ghost aware that she is dead? Maybe she feels so odd in spirit form that she assumes she is sick.

While Florence's story is fascinating, it was not the only tragedy that played out at the Oxford. My digging also unearthed another bit of dirt. In the summer of 1937, notorious German-born killer Anna Marie Hahn passed through Denver with her twelve-year-old son and her latest groaning victim in tow. George Obendoerfer, sixty-seven, had been fed an arsenic-laced sandwich by the murderess on the train to the city. She and her ailing victim checked into the Oxford for a brief stay before moving on. While the poor man soon died elsewhere, he spent some of his last tormented hours in the grand hotel.

Thirty-two-year-old "Arsenic Anna," became America's first woman serial killer to fry in the electric chair on December 7, 1938.

While documented accounts of violence at the Oxford Hotel are tough enough to find, odds are that most of the drama that occurred there was never recorded—except, perhaps *by the walls*. If it weren't for the ethereal figures that float through the doors, dance in the mirrors, and wake up the guests, those who lived and died there would be long forgotten.

THE OXFORD HOTEL
1600 Seventeenth Street
Denver, Colorado 80202
(303) 628-5400
www.theoxfordhotel.com

Haunted Hotels

IN THE NEWS

The Windsor Hotel

On August 11, 2006, *WALB News 10* got the scoop on the haunting at an Americus, Georgia, hotel. A reporter interviewed the dining room manager, Ida Robinson, who said she had once encountered a ghost in an upstairs hallway. The figure raced past her as she was delivering a tray of food.

On June 16, 1892, the Windsor Hotel opened its doors to thousands of eager people who flocked to town to admire the building with its turrets and towers and rows of arched windows. It is not just the extravagant architecture that attracts guests. Many visit in hopes of seeing ghosts.

Adventuresome guests book rooms on the third floor where the spirits are most often seen. Hotel legend says that the daughter of a maid was pushed down an elevator shaft in the early 1900s. The child's ghost is said to be seen giggling as she runs down the halls.

Other paranormal activity includes pots and pans moving by themselves and the startling sound of disembodied voices.

The television station also revealed that the Windsor was scheduled to be investigated by paranormal experts, the Big Bend Ghost Trackers.

Another news account from the *Americus Times-Recorder* later detailed the investigation. The highlight of the evening was the sighting of the silhouette of the late Floyd Lowery on the third floor. A forty-year employee of the Windsor, Floyd was a doorman who also ran the elevator.

THE WINDSOR HOTEL
125 W. Lamar Street
Americus, Georgia 31709
(229) 924-1555

THE ROGERS HOTEL

Newspapers in Waxahachie, Texas, describe spooky happenings at the Rogers Hotel. The twenty-seven-room inn, named for Waxahachie founder and original hotel owner Emory W. Rogers, who once lived in a log cabin near the spot, is home to a number of spirits.

Premature deaths of a few of the Rogers family members are believed to account for some of the earthbound entities.

The hotel was destroyed twice in fires, once in 1881 and again in 1911. Stephen A. Clift helped fight the first fire and died as a result of smoke-induced paralysis. Some wonder if he may be responsible for the activity in room 409.

Guests who stay in that room have confessed to waking up to find an apparition of a cowboy standing over the bed. Some believe the cowboy is the ghost of a man who allegedly hanged himself in that room. The suicide victim is thought to be the son of a former owner.

A mysterious little girl with long, dark hair also manifests at the hotel. Staff report seeing her most often in the restaurant area and in the boiler room. Rumors say that she drowned in a mineral pool in the basement of the building.

Employees are also startled by such things as cushions pulled off of the sofa by unseen hands, magazines thrown to the ground, and phantom music emanating from room 202.

Sources include:
Waxahachie Daily Light *June 30, 2007*
Star-Telegram *October 28, 2007*

THE ROGERS HOTEL
100 N. College
Waxahachie, Texas 75165
(927) 938-3688
www.rogershotel.com

Hotel Ghosts

The Brown Palace

Ever since it opened its doors on August 12, 1892, the Brown Palace Hotel in Denver, Colorado, has catered to the elite. Elegant and extravagant, the Italian Renaissance–style structure occupies a triangular plot in downtown Denver where original owner Henry Cords Brown once grazed his cow. The atrium lobby soars past eight floors of interior balconies and the eye is naturally drawn to the cast-iron railings on each level.

Guests have included a number of U.S. presidents, including Dwight Eisenhower, who maintained a summertime headquarters there throughout his presidency. "Ike" literally made an impression upon the hotel when he was practicing his golf swing in his room. The ball struck the fireplace mantel and dented it. Rather than repair the mantel, management proudly preserved the dent as a presidential souvenir.

Others, too, have made impressions upon the place, some that hotel management wishes they could forget. History, however, is set, and no matter how much we want to forget it, we cannot change it.

The Brown Palace saw tragedy on May 24, 1911. The bar beside the hotel's Broadway entrance was the scene of a murder long in the making. The convoluted drama was scrutinized in newspapers throughout the nation and was recently chronicled in journalist Dick Kreck's book *Murder at the Brown Palace: A True Story of Seduction and Betrayal.*

A seemingly helpless female guest pulled the strings of her hapless, smitten puppets. Her name was Isabel Springer and though she was married to wealthy politician John W. Springer, she carried on with two other men.

Sylvester "Tony" Von Phul was a celebrated St. Louis, Missouri, hot air balloon pilot who traveled to the Brown Palace after receiving letters from Isabel begging him to meet her there for an intimate reunion.

The site of a century old murderous scandal, this Denver luxury hotel caters to both the living and the dead. (Leslie Rule)

Many years ago, nets were hung beneath the balconies to prevent distraught Brown Palace guests from leaping to their deaths. (Leslie Rule)

Meanwhile, she was lying to another suitor, entrepreneur Frank Henwood. She told him that Tony had threatened to blackmail her unless she continued her relationship with him.

While living with her husband in a sixth-floor suite at the Brown Palace, Isabel manipulated the three men who adored her.

After weeks of lies, the tension escalated. Tony and Frank faced off in the Brown Palace barroom. Frank drew a gun and shot at Von Phul, who fell to the floor and died within hours. Two innocent bystanders were also hit. One was killed while the other was critically injured.

Many lives were ruined, including Isabel's. Her husband left her when the truth came out in court. A few years later, she died a pauper.

Frank died in prison at age fifty-two in 1929.

Many have reported seeing ghosts at the hotel, and the management encourages the stories, though they don't like to talk about the Springer tragedy.

Witnesses have seen the ghost of a porter in the hotel lobby, and an apparition of a man in a bathtub in one of the rooms.

Electronic voice phenomena (EVP) expert Debby Constantino knew nothing of the hotel's history when she captured a phantom voice of a male on tape saying, "Got you both."

Perhaps it was the ghost of one of the shooting victims, talking to the two others who were shot that night.

THE BROWN PALACE HOTEL AND SPA
321 17th Street
Denver, Colorado 80202
(303) 297-3111
www.brownpalace.com

Florida Fright

Employees of a luxurious Florida beach resort report ghostly activity in their historic building. Opened in 1928 and dubbed the Pink Palace because of its

This luxurious Florida hotel once served as a veteran's hospital. Some believe that the ghosts of patients still walk the halls. (Leslie Rule)

distinctive color, the Don CeSar in St. Petersburg Beach housed a veterans hospital during the 1940s.

While legend has it that the ghost of the hotel's founder, Thomas Rowe, is responsible for the paranormal activity, the restless spirits of ailing soldiers may contribute to the haunting. Many veterans spent time in the psychiatric ward for combat fatigue and went to their graves with troubled hearts.

Anne Douglass, a retail clerk in the basement gift shop, was skeptical before her encounter with an unseen entity. "I have two degrees in math and science," she told me, explaining that she had previously dismissed the idea of ghosts as a fanciful notion.

One night she was alone in the shop when a purse flew off a shelf with such force she had to duck when she saw it coming toward her. "It didn't just fall," she said. "It was projected through the air."

The swimming pool captures the reflection of the haunted hotel. (Leslie Rule)

Security guard David Mogren had his most chilling experience on his very first night on the job. Another guard was showing him around and as they approached an outside stairwell, they heard a weird sound.

"It was a loud rumbling, and it came from the stairwell," David told me.

The other guard turned pale, and said, "Let's get out of here!"

"There was no logical explanation for the noise and I've never heard it since that night," said David.

All three of these employees have experienced paranormal activity at the Don CeSar. (Leslie Rule)

Hotel security guard David Mogren stands on the stairwell where he once heard something very strange. (Leslie Rule)

Banquet captain Reggie Bumbray confided he once saw a shadowy figure in one of the resort offices. "Someone tapped me on my shoulder," he said. When he turned around, there was no one there.

In her twenty years at the Don CeSar, Marion Martin has become aware of the ghosts. She has heard a phantom voice call her name in a back stairway used by employees. The stair area is especially creepy, according to Marion, who told me, "Sometimes it feels as if a cold breeze is blowing through the stairwell."

Hundreds of famous people have stayed at this luxury hotel, though not all were aware that they were among restless spirits. (Leslie Rule)

Pampered guests at the Don CeSar don't seem to mind sharing their lush surroundings with ghosts. (Leslie Rule)

Though a warm breeze blows outside of the Don CeSar, a ghostly chill sometimes gives sunbathers gooseflesh. (Leslie Rule)

Even on hot, windless days, the icy gust can be felt on the stairs.

Cambric Lawson was setting up for a banquet in the King Charles Ballroom on the fifth floor of the resort when he heard footsteps in the huge, empty room. "It happened twice within three weeks," he told me, adding that the incidents occurred when he was new on the job.

DON CESAR BEACH RESORT
3400 Gulf Boulevard
St. Petersburg Beach, Florida 33706
(813) 360-1881
www.doncesar.com

Ghosts of the Grand Lodge

Some employees of the Grand Lodge in Forest Grove, Oregon, are afraid to go to the hotel's basement, the most haunted area of the 1917 structure. Both guests and staff report a "creepy feeling" in the bowels of the building, as if they are being watched.

The Grand Lodge in Forest Grove, Oregon, is a favorite destination for ghost enthusiasts. (Leslie Rule)

Built as a Masonic and Eastern Star Home, the Grand Lodge was once filled with "the old and the infirmed," while the adjacent building served as an orphanage.

Spirits of past residents have been seen throughout the property. A front desk clerk told me that she had once seen the apparition of an old gentleman. He stood at the top of the second-floor staircase and slowly faded away.

A log of the ghostly activity is kept at the front desk and visitors are encouraged to record their experiences.

In January of 2008, a couple was staying in room 003 in the basement when the man felt someone tap him on his shoulder. He asked his girlfriend why she had tapped him. "I didn't," she said. Then they heard the sound of feet shuffling across the floor, as if an unseen visitor was walking away.

THE GRAND LODGE
3505 Pacific Avenue
Forest Grove, Oregon 97116
(503) 992-9533
www.thegrandlodge.com

5

HUNGRY AND HAUNTED

I have been to dozens of haunted restaurants in my quest to find ghost stories. While I always hope that I will see a spirit, I don't hold my breath. I know that such encounters are usually spontaneous and happen when we least expect them.

I was definitely not thinking of spirits when I had my oddest experience in a haunted restaurant. In fact, I was not there to research a book and was not aware that the place had a ghost. It was late December 2007, and a group of us had gathered at Germaine's Country Kitchen in Burien, Washington, for an emergency fund-raiser for a homeless cat shelter.

The restaurant owners had volunteered the use of their place and made cake and coffee for the guests. Halfway through the evening I ducked into the back to look for the owner. As I stepped into the kitchen, I saw a flurry of movement from the corner of my eye and turned to see what I assumed was the door to the walk-in refrigerator.

I figured that I had glimpsed the owner as she entered the walk-in. I was about to follow her when a dust pan, tucked between the walk-in and the wall, suddenly dropped about four inches.

Instinctively, I touched it. It was wedged tightly in the spot. There was no way that the dust pan had simply shifted. It would have taken considerable muscle to force it into the space. I then realized that the walk-in refrigerator was not a walk-in, after all. It was a regular, small fridge.

I kicked myself for not turning my head fast enough. I had just missed seeing the Germaine's Country Kitchen Ghost. I later learned that others have sensed a male presence in the spot.

Many people in haunted eateries have had spirit encounters far more involved than mine.

GERMAINE'S COUNTRY KITCHEN
15321 First Avenue S.
Burien, Washington 98148
(206) 244-3100

THURSDAY'S GHOST

When customers use the ladies' room at Café Batavia, they are sometimes startled when they glance into the mirror and see a stranger standing behind them.

According to an owner of the Kota, Jakarta, Indonesian restaurant, the beautiful woman with the long dark hair and red dress most often materializes on Thursday nights.

The owner and I have been e-mail friends since 2001, shortly after she read my first book of true ghost stories and she has kept me posted on the paranormal activity in the popular restaurant.

The Thursday ghost often appears in the mirrors of this classy restaurant. (courtesy of Cafe Batavia)

Both customers and employees have encountered the ghost, who also manifests in the hallways of the elegant restaurant. The spirit is a lady of many moods. Some witnesses have reported that she is laughing, while others have seen tears streaming down her cheeks. The apparition usually appears for a full five seconds before vanishing.

Who is she?

"The building dates to the early 1800s," said Café Batavia's co-owner, who noted that the nearby Fatahillah Museum may be the source of the haunting. "The museum had at one time been the site of offices in the Dutch era," she said. "Later, it was occupied by the Japanese. We've heard rumors that people were tortured and killed there. We think that the ghost may have left that building and taken refuge here."

The Thursday ghost is not the only one seen in Café Batavia. Witnesses have also seen the ghosts of two different men. In addition, employees are stunned to find that the bathroom doors mysteriously lock themselves, toilets flush on their own, and the printer and photo-copy machine frequently turn themselves on.

The restaurant owners say that the weirdest thing of all occurs during staff meetings when an employee is absent. Witnesses will often see the missing employee somewhere on the premises, only to learn that that person is at home. "It is the ghost," said one of the owners, "taking the form of the absent staff member."

CAFÉ BATAVIA
Kota, Jakarta, Indonesia
www.cafebatavia.com

TRAPPED IN TACOMA

Theresa Ricon took a break during a quiet time at Alfred's Café in Tacoma, Washington. As she sat down to enjoy a few moments of rest between customers, she glanced at the mirror and noticed someone at one of her tables.

"When I got up to wait on them, I realized that no one was there," said the part-time waitress and mother of two young children. She shivered a little as she told me the story. "It scares me," she admitted, as she glanced around at the mirrors in the historic building.

Every inch of the walls of the popular restaurant and the adjoining diner is covered with mirrors. They reflect back upon each other endlessly in a dramatic effect that enlarges the space and, perhaps, creates a passage for ghosts.

Housed in a one-time hotel on Puyallup Avenue, a few blocks from the icy waters of Puget Sound, Alfred's Café serves up classic

American food on the ground floor while the two upper floors are used for storage.

Opened in 1888 as the Hotel Brunswick, the three-story building originally sat a couple of blocks up the hill, beside the train station. The building was moved in 1907.

While it is easy to find old postcards of other historic hotels in town, apparently none were printed of the Brunswick. It seems that

Employees have seen apparitions in the mirrors of this Tacoma, Washington, restaurant. (Leslie Rule)

customers were not eager to write home and brag about their stay there. Perhaps they did not want their friends and relatives to know that they were visiting a *brothel*.

The hotel, tucked discreetly next to the railroad tracks, was not the most reputable place in town. During an era when proper ladies' skirts swished about their ankles and divorce was a scandal, the secrets within the walls of the Hotel Brunswick would have shocked the respectable citizens of Tacoma.

The hotel's second and third floors were chopped into small rooms, none much larger than a horse's stable. There, the liquor flowed freely and the women were not shy.

Over a century later, the rooms are still intact, complete with their original doors and transom windows. Worn linoleum and aged wallpaper, installed sometime around the 1930s, remain in place. Old wiring and new fire codes prevent the owners from opening the space to the public.

Today, the upper floors are a dusty place. Some of the tiny rooms are empty, while others are filled with tangled heaps of chairs and various dining artifacts. The storage room is clean and tidy, stacked with huge cans of the standard restaurant staples.

"I don't like to go upstairs," Theresa told me. And she is not alone in her apprehension. Some other employees have also refused to venture upstairs alone.

It is usually the dishwashers' job to fetch supplies. They must adhere to the task at hand and try not to think about the mysterious noises that emanate from above. For sometimes, the staff is startled by the sudden, loud clomping of footsteps, and the thud of objects falling to the floor. "We'll look around and see that all of the dishwashers are accounted for," said Theresa. "We realize that no one is upstairs."

Employees shudder and shoot each other knowing glances as they try to concentrate on taking orders or mixing drinks. Braver employees have searched for the source of the noise and are baffled to find nothing out of place.

Who are the ghosts of the old Brunswick Hotel?

Some may be from the days of the brothel, while others may have visited or worked in the building during another era. For many years, a popular tavern occupied the ground floor. A bartender who died decades ago has materialized in the restaurant. A waitress reported that she arrived in the morning to see the fellow standing behind the bar.

An Alfred's bartender told me that things inexplicably disappear from the place. "Right now, we're missing the chore book," he said. "It lists side work and the waitresses check off the jobs they complete each day. It's been missing for a few days."

He also admitted that he has closed the place up at night, and turned off all of the lights, only to return in the morning to find the lights blazing.

Whoever haunts the place likes to tease the waitresses. Rebecca Sheiman was behind the bar after closing one night when she felt a sharp tug on her hair. "I turned around and there was no one there," she said.

Theresa Ricon was in the same area when she felt someone pull on her apron strings. While a number of spirits may linger in the historic structure for a variety of reasons, at least one may be grounded in sorrow. A former cook saw her and told Theresa about it. "The cook left the month I started here," she said, as she recalled the frightened awe in his voice as he confided in her.

He had gone upstairs for supplies. When he passed the foot of the open antique staircase on the second floor, he glanced up: A woman in a long skirt was standing on the third-floor landing. He glimpsed her for only a moment but a few details registered. Not only was her outfit from the early part of the twentieth century, but the area around her was also from a bygone era.

"He saw pictures on the walls," Theresa said.

The cook was stunned by the image from long ago. His eyes were drawn to the woman's slender white arms that were covered in bruises. The scenario vanished before he had time to question it.

His shocking encounter gives us a poignant clue to the identity of one of the building's ghosts. The woman had been abused, and most likely, worked in the brothel. She was probably at the mercy of the strangers who visited her in her confined room. She may have been killed by one of the patrons, her body tossed in Puget Sound and lost forever in the vast, salty depths. *If* anyone had cared enough to report her missing, she would not have been a high priority on the detectives' agenda. The loud disturbances the employees heard could very well be the sound of her attacker beating her.

The image the cook saw and the sounds that the others heard could also be the result of a phenomenon known as a place memory, also called a residual haunting.

In this type of odd occurrence, it is theorized that a dramatic event is inexplicably recorded by the environment—only to be played back at a later date and witnessed by others.

If this is the case, the bruised woman may or may not have been killed. Whatever the circumstances, if the event was indeed a residual haunting, the woman seen was not a conscious entity able to interact, but only an *image* of an event from long ago. The fact that the cook also noted that the area around her was from another era, would strongly point to the possibility that he experienced a place memory rather than an actual spirit.

ALFRED'S CAFÉ ·
402 Puyallup Avenue
Tacoma, Washington 98421
(253) 627-5491

SPOOKED IN DENVER

When it comes to working the late shift in a Rioja's in Denver's Larimer Square, few employees are brave enough to work alone.

The restaurant, housed on the first floor of a historic building at 1431 Larimer Street, has long been the site of ghostly activity. After the last customer has left and waitresses have counted their tips, disembodied footsteps clomp over the gleaming hardwood floors, and fragments of conversation from another era waft from nowhere to punctuate the silence.

The business, known as Josephina's Italian Restaurant for thirty-one years, went through several owners and countless employees before the last pot of spaghetti sauce was stirred in 2005. The previous year the space had been divided in two, with an award-winning chef teaming up with a savvy businesswoman to open Rioja's on the other side of the wall. The new restaurant opened but it inherited at least one ghost.

Since it was erected in 1901, the three-story brick building has housed a variety of businesses, including a barbershop, secondhand stores, and a corset shop. The upper floors once served as the Frontenac Hotel and later became offices. Much of the history of those who came and went has been forgotten, yet stubborn spirits cling to the ground floor.

When I dined at Rioja's, I learned that a waitress had seen the apparition of a pretty young woman in an old-time dress standing at the end of the bar.

My waitress eagerly shared the story of Amelia, the restaurant's ghost, who supposedly once lived in the building with her husband and daughter, Ginger. Ginger's parents did not approve of her choice of suitor and had him killed. In the end both Ginger and Amelia died tragically—one from heartbreak, the other from suicide.

The case, however, is undocumented. Although repeated many times and picked up by the media, the Amelia story is just a legend. It came from an unnamed psychic who supplied the entire scenario, complete with names. If she was accurate, I have yet to find anything to support it. Maybe she found a thread of truth, or maybe she simply had a good imagination.

While I am suspicious of the Amelia story, I did not have to look far to find a possible source for the haunting.

Larimer Street is the oldest street in Denver. It all began in 1858 when gold was discovered at the confluence of Cherry Creek and the South Platte River. General William Larimer arrived soon after. He ignored a claim made by others and staked his own town site. The young men who had arrived first were intimidated by the middle-aged general and gave in to his bullying. The general named the city after Kansas Territory Governor James Denver and Larimer Street for himself.

He built a home: an approximate sixteen-by-sixteen-foot log cabin. It showed off the city's first glass window and occupied a spot at 1460 Larimer. Eerily, the doors of the home were actually coffin lids. It was a macabre statement on a street that would one day be a path for death and ghosts.

My search of newspaper archives turned up countless cases of violence and suicides on Larimer Street in the late 1800s and early 1900s, including several stories of women who died after swallowing poison.

An April 1890 article in the *Freeborn County Standard* reported a disturbing incident:

April 3, Count Schimmerman Von Hartman, of Hamburg, Germany, walked into a saloon on Larimer Street on Tuesday and deliberately drawing a revolver, placed the muzzle to his head and blew

his brains out in the presence of a half-dozen spectators. Poverty and
drink were the causes attributed to the suicide.

While some on Larimer died by their own hand, others had help. An old cottonwood tree near 1400 and Larimer served as a hanging tree where many unruly citizens were executed. It was just one more example of sorrow and violence that would leave its gloomy mark on the street.

In the early 1900s, Larimer Street fell into disrepair and few appreciated its historic significance. It became Denver's Skid Row, with the run-down buildings providing cheap rent for unsavory business with criminals, alcoholics, and drug addicts for clientele.

The old buildings were nearly demolished, but preservationists stepped in and saved them, beginning with the structures on the 1400 block, which was placed on the National Register of Historic Places in 1973. The section, known as Larimer Square, has been restored and is now a classy place, rife with upscale shops, acclaimed eateries, and busy bars.

Rioja's fits right in. Chris Sullivan helped to transform the restaurant when he installed the wood floor during the 2004 remodel. The owner of his own flooring business, the thirty-three-year-old is proud of his work at Rioja's but he refuses to do another job there. "I don't want to be in that building alone ever again," he said, adding that he had to hire friends to keep him company when he installed the floor after he got spooked.

"I heard loud popping sounds," he said. "It sounded like two boards slamming together." He tried to shrug off the noises, but a trip to the men's room left him shaken.

It was about 7:00 p.m. as he walked down the dim hallway toward the restroom when a woman crossed his path. "She was right in front of the mirror and she wore a beige Victorian dress," he confided. The sighting was followed by an icy blast. "I'm a hairy guy," Chris said. "And all of the hairs on my arms and the back of my neck were standing up."

Rattled, he went for coffee to calm himself down, leaving his cousin Derrick to work alone. When he returned he found Derrick on the sidewalk, the door to the restaurant wide open, and over a dozen people wandering through the restaurant.

"The sidewalks were covered with snow and they were tracking it all over the floor," said Chris. As politely as possible, he informed the group that the floor was not yet finished and ushered them out.

Before he could reprimand Derrick for letting the crowd in, his cousin told him, "I just got the weirdest feeling. I had to get out of there!"

Chris had kept his experience to himself so when he saw how frightened his cousin was it validated his sense that something strange was going on. He does not know if the ghosts of Rioja's stay put or if they are also responsible for the activity in the Clayton Building across the street.

The Clayton was built in 1882 on the spot where Larimer erected his cabin, and the structure once served as the Granite Hotel. According to Chris the place is also paranormally active. At least two shocked witnesses have seen the apparition of a little girl tap dancing in the building. "She is transparent and she usually appears on the third floor," he said. "She looks like she is about eight years old."

The child may have lived in the building and taken lessons at the nearby dance school. Mrs. White's Dance Academy occupied the spot at 1415 Larimer around the year 1900. The school featured a suspended floor, a contraption that allowed for more bounce. It was a stone's throw from the building where the ghostly child is seen.

In his 1982 book, *Denver's Larimer Street*, historian Thomas J. Noel wrote that the dancing school was "notorious for drunkenness, disorder, and debauching of young women and girls who came to the dances. Josephine Roche, Denver's first policewoman and other officials closed it down on various occasions."

The dance school was several doors down from the building that today houses Rioja's. The old dance academy may very well be the source for some of the drama that inspires the ghosts who swarm Larimer Square.

RIOJA'S
1431 Larimer Street
Denver, Colorado 80202
(303) 820-2282
www.riojadenver.com

MATTIE'S HOUSE OF MIRRORS

Sadie. Hattie. Lottie. Nellie. These are some of the young ladies listed as "boarders" by the 1900 United States Census report. They lived under the roof of "landlady" Mattie Silks at a notorious Market Street address in Denver, Colorado.

"The oldest profession" was as depressing, dangerous, and degrading for women then as it is today. Suicides in seedy Denver were not rare, and some were associated with Madam Mattie Silks.

"Mattie's House of Mirrors" featured a mirrored lobby and a restaurant popular with men. The women she employed roomed on the second floor. Mattie Silks claimed to be thirty-five years old in 1900, but records indicate she was much older. She was definitely older and wiser than the girls she enticed into the sordid life of prostitution. Historians note a spirited competition between Mattie and the other madams who ran brothels in the neighborhood. It is unlikely that these pimps of yesteryear felt much guilt in leading teenaged girls down a pathetic path. Smooth skin and wide, innocent eyes were simply a commodity to be traded. When the skin sagged and the light went out of the eyes, the women were discarded.

Eventually, as moral reform swept the nation, Denver's brothels were closed down. By 1920 Mattie's was long gone. The narrow, three-story brick building housed a number of establishments over the years, including a Buddhist temple, a bicycle repair shop, and a barbershop.

The tenants may have come and gone, but for the women who lived and died there at the turn of the century, time stands still. Perhaps they slept for a while, but stirred again when the place recently became a restaurant and the name was restored. It began with a flicker of lights. "The owner noticed it one quiet night," said historian Kevin Rucker of LoDo Historic Walking Tours. "It was right before closing, and the lights were dimming and brightening with the cadence of his breath."

The historian also told me about a restless lady who paced in a room on the second floor. She walked back and forth past the upstairs left-hand window. Passersby couldn't help but notice her as they glanced up at the lit window at night. "The owner got numerous phone calls from people who had seen her," he said.

Who is the agitated spirit? Maybe she is a victim. Women in brothels were vulnerable to violence. A sudden disappearance did not warrant much of an investigation and many females were victims of homicides never reported. The ghosts of ladies murdered in Denver's red-light district may still lurk in the area.

Ella Wellington is another sad figure and a definite candidate for a House of Mirrors ghost. Archives show her as onetime proprietor of the House of Mirrors, with newspaper accounts referring to the place as "a resort."

A Saturday, July 28, 1894, edition of Hamilton, Ohio's *Hamilton Daily Republican* reported on a Denver tragedy:

> *Mrs. Ella Wellington committed suicide here Friday by sending a bullet through her brain. She separated from her husband in Omaha three years ago, and sent her children to Boston to be educated. She opened a costly resort on Market Street, and possessed $30,000 worth of jewels. Her act is attributed to melancholy on account of her domestic troubles.*

Another newspaper noted that Ella was thirty-one years old and depressed because of her separation from her children.

Bryan Bonner of the Rocky Mountain Paranormal Research Society has been investigating the House of Mirrors since December 11, 2000. He considers historical research a valuable aspect of the endeavor. Aware of Ella's suicide, he has also been trying to document another suicide rumored to have taken place on the premises.

"He was a boyfriend of one of Mattie's girls," Bryan told me. "We think he hanged himself near the restrooms on the second floor."

During their initial investigation, Bryan's group discovered an anomaly on the very spot where the man purportedly died. As a team member mentioned the man and the suicide, a light on the wall began an odd display of dimming and brightening.

"The light on the wall is on the same circuit as the one on the ceiling," Bryan explained. While the ceiling light remained steady, the wall light seemed to pulsate, astonishing the witnesses.

In addition to the curious light show, the group also noted that the elevator moved from floor to floor on its own, the video camera was repeatedly turned off, and the hanging lights swayed for no discernable reason.

Bryan is still puzzled by another strange piece of evidence. The group recorded a phantom voice, speaking in a language that has so far stumped linguistic experts.

"Paranormal activity has been reported in the place for years. Most of it seems to be on the second floor," said Bryan who interviewed the staff at the House of Mirrors about their personal experiences.

Some employees are so spooked that they refuse to go to the second floor by themselves. The piano there plays on its own, as if phantom fingers are tiptoeing over the keys. Bartenders told Bryan that they have even seen ghostly faces reflected in the bar mirror.

Perhaps it is Ella, materializing in the mirror, or maybe it is Mattie Woods. Before Mattie Silks, another Mattie lived and died nearby.

I discovered Mattie Woods during archival research. In an 1880 census report, she surfaced as the twenty-two-year-old English-born head of a household on Holladay Street—the former name for Market Street. She obviously ran a brothel. The "boarders" were all young women and the street had a tawdry reputation. The record was damaged and the exact street number was hard to decipher, but it looked like 502. I do not know if the house numbers were changed with the street names so I cannot determine the proximity of the location to the site of today's House of Mirrors.

The Matties, however, were connected. For the *Colorado Springs Daily Gazette* reported that Mattie Woods killed herself on March 1, 1881, by taking chloroform at "Mattie Silks's house of ill fame."

While the suicide came seven years before the opening of the House of Mirrors, the poor young woman was a victim of the despair of Denver's downtrodden and a contender as a brothel ghost.

Paranormal researchers theorize that spirits can attach themselves to possessions and it is within the realm of possibilities that Mattie Woods moved with the furniture from Mattie Silks's old place to her new celebrated House of Mirrors. Today Mattie's House of Mirrors is a banquet hall, available for private catered affairs.

Most of Mattie's original mirrors are gone, but the ghosts once reflected there remain.

MATTIE'S HOUSE OF MIRRORS RESTAURANT, BAR, AND BANQUET HALL
1946 Market Street
Denver, Colorado 80202
(303) 297-9600
www.mattieshouseofmirrors.com

THE WINE CELLAR

Tiny lizards bathe in the sunshine in the garden outside. Palm trees shiver in the tropical breeze—a salty, warm wind that blows from the gulf across the busy boulevard.

The Wine Cellar in North Redington Beach, Florida, does not look like a haunted place. Few would guess that the classy restaurant harbors a restless spirit.

The Wine Cellar features a cozy dining room with subdued lighting where attentive waiters in tailored suits serve both "traditional and multicultural cuisine" prepared by critically acclaimed chefs.

"I always said that I did not believe in ghosts," said Christina Brignall, whose parents have owned the restaurant on the Gulf of Mexico for over three decades. Yet she cannot dismiss the strange things that occurred while she was managing the place a decade and a half ago.

It started when employees told her the place was haunted. Christina laughed it off, until the afternoon she and a couple of members of the wait staff were alone in the restaurant after closing. As she sat at the bar, chatting with the others, someone brought up ghosts. "I don't believe in ghosts," Christina stated.

The instant the words left her mouth, the light over her head went off. "Lights run down the ceiling in a row over the bar, and it was the only one that went out," she told me. "It was directly over my head."

A moment later, she reconsidered and said, "I guess I kind of believe." The light instantly came back on as the group tittered nervously.

Another time as she was visiting with employees after work they were startled by the familiar sound of someone stacking dishes. "We looked around but there was no one there but us," she said.

Today Christina is a wife and mother who lives in Kalamazoo, Michigan. Though still an admitted skeptic, she cannot forget an odd encounter in the Wine Cellar's kitchen. "I was locking up after closing when I saw a foggy shadow," she confided. "At first I thought it was steam coming from the dishwasher."

Employees sometimes encounter a desperate spirit within the walls of the Wine Cellar. (Leslie Rule)

Though the exit is clearly marked, one former worker cannot find his way out. (Leslie Rule)

But the dishwasher had been turned off and had cooled down. The "steam" took on the vague shape of a human form. "I was startled and I backed up a step."

The hairs on her forearms prickled to attention. She had just seen a ghost and she knew who it was. A few years earlier a man named Eliseo had worked as their janitor. He was a conscientious, older gentleman. "He died in the service bar. My sister found him," said Christina. "I think he had a heart attack."

The poor man had been working alone when he passed away. And though he passed *away* he, apparently, has not passed *on*. The noise of clattering dishes still emanates from the empty banquet rooms, and sometimes the staff finds that the table settings have been mysteriously rearranged.

An employee was recently spooked when he discovered silverware laid out in a most unusual fashion. He swears that after he had set the tables, no one else had access to the banquet room. Yet when he returned, he found that the shiny utensils had been rearranged to spell two chilling words. *Help me.*

THE WINE CELLAR
17307 Gulf Boulevard
North Redington Beach, Florida 33708
(727) 393-3491
www.thewinecellar.com

OUT OF PLACE

Rino Ouellet does not believe in ghosts. He has been manager of J. Timothy's Taverne in Plainville, Connecticut, for eighteen years, and is well aware of its reputation as a haunted place. "It's a fun, old building," he said, acknowledging that he's heard both employees and customers share stories about disembodied footsteps and phantom voices inside the authentic New England tavern.

Despite his skepticism, Rino admitted that he sometimes hears himself say good night to Mrs. Cooke when he leaves in the evening.

Mrs. Cooke has been dead for a very long time. She was the owner of Cooke's Tavern, and had operated the place when it was the hub of Connecticut's social scene. The tavern opened in 1789, the same year George Washington became president, and local legend says that he slept there—or at the very least enjoyed a hearty meal there.

The structure housed a tavern for two centuries, and has had plenty of time to collect spirits. "There is a lot of lore associated with the building," Rino Ouellet told me. "And there has been death in the building."

According to Rino, a recent employee was a shirttail relative of a murder victim who had once worked there. He had been the night custodian and was killed inside the building. "I think it was in the 1940s," he told me.

While the poor guy is a good candidate for a ghost, he probably is not the spirit seen by Jenna Gomes, a high school girl who saw an apparition of a man in eighteenth-century garb. "I went to dinner there with my friend, Rachel Cutler," said Jenna, a Farmington, Connecticut, teen. "We were standing in the entryway, waiting to be seated when Rachel pointed to someone standing by the fireplace in the next room. I assumed that she was pointing at an oddly dressed man who stood alone as he stared off into the distance."

Jenna found the fellow fascinating. He wore a navy blazer with tails and a big white collar. He looked about forty and his pale skin stood out in stark contrast to his black hair and beard.

"I was surprised that no one else was paying attention to him," Jenna told me. "He was so out of place. Everyone just walked by him as if he wasn't there. Rachel mumbled something that I couldn't quite hear and she headed across the room to ask someone a question. As she walked away, the strange man left the fireplace area, crossing in front of me as he headed into the next room."

The peculiar stranger entered another room, vanishing from sight. "I had a clear view of the room," she said. "He actually disappeared!"

Stunned, Jenna tried to tell Rachel about what she had seen. "That weird guy just *vanished*," she cried.

"What weird guy?" asked Rachel.

"The man by the fireplace. The man you pointed to," Jenna replied.

Rachel shook her head and said, "I was pointing to the waitress. I didn't see anyone by the fireplace."

The girls were spooked, yet they wondered if Jenna's eyes had played a trick on her. "We searched the restaurant, even sneaking into the men's room and peeking into the kitchen," she said. "We couldn't find him."

How had the man slipped away so quickly? And why hadn't Rachel seen him when he stood out so dramatically?

Jenna could not forget the strange man and his vacant stare so she and Rachel soon returned to the restaurant, bringing a camera with them. While they were in the ladies' room, Jenna snapped a photo of her friend as she stood by the sink.

When they looked at the photograph, they were taken aback. Instead of Rachel's pretty face, they saw a sharp-faced crone with dark circles for eyes. They took more photos in the restroom for comparison, but those all appeared normal. They were not able to re-create the anomaly. Maybe it was just a trick of the light, or maybe a ghostly face superimposed itself over Rachel's face.

J. TIMOTHY'S TAVERNE
143 New Britain Avenue
Plainville, Connecticut 06062
(860) 747-6813
www.jtimothys.com

THE DOCTOR IS IN

"Here they come!"

It was the voice of a child, innocent and whispering and caught on tape. John Chavez felt a chill when he heard it. The phrase, he said, had been repeated three times by a ghostly child and recorded by the paranormal researchers he had invited to investigate the haunted restaurant.

As manager of the elegant Anaheim White House Restaurant in Anaheim, California, John is both fascinated and spooked by the mischievous entities who play tricks on his staff.

❧

Long before Walt Disney drew his first cartoon mouse, Anaheim was a peaceful place. The air was tinged with the tangy scent of oranges from the groves that grew on the rolling hills.

When Dosithe Gervais built the lovely mansion in 1909, he could not have imagined that the area would one day be sliced up by con-

crete roadways where metallic automobiles of every color sped by;
many headed toward a world-famous amusement park where visitors waiting at the entrance could quickly outnumber the city's entire
population.

Today the mansion still stands, and while the world around it
barely resembles that of a century ago, time has remained frozen for

A deceased doctor may be behind the haunting at this Anaheim, California, restaurant. (Leslie Rule)

those who hide in its shadows. The ghosts of the Anaheim White House Restaurant may still see the world through eyes of yesteryear.

The restaurant offers first-class service from waiters with perky bow ties and entrees prepared by award-winning chefs.

My meal at the Anaheim White House Restaurant called for a nice tip. I reached into my purse and doled out enough for Anaheim's settlers to purchase fifteen acres of land.

As a former waitress I *am* a generous tipper, though not as generous as it appears. Anaheim's first citizens paid *two dollars per acre*. German winemakers founded the place in 1857, naming it Anaheim, German for "home (*heim*) by the river."

Several decades later, a blight destroyed the vineyards and, consequently, the area's wine business. Citrus fruits were cultivated and by the time the 1909 mansion was built, orange groves filled the land. The big house sat in the middle of acres of orange trees.

The Waterman family purchased the gracious home in 1916. Shortly after, Dr. John Truxaw and his wife, Louise, bought the place and raised their family there. A beloved obstetrician, Dr. Truxaw brought over 3,500 babies into the world. Everyone recognized his small, white Buick coupe, as he hurried off to deliver another infant.

Dr. and Mrs. Truxaw lived in the home for half a century. The community mourned when Dr. Truxaw died in October 1952, at age sixty-nine. His wife died in a convalescent hospital at age seventy-seven on November 11, 1969.

The house then became a rental, and in 1977 it was leased by an organization catering to "reformed" alcoholics who had little respect for the grand, old home. The tenants ripped cupboards from the walls and burned them in the fireplace. They punched and kicked holes in the walls, and littered the floors with empty wine bottles and garbage.

While most potential buyers thought the home was beyond repair, Mrs. Anthony Bouck purchased the place in 1978, with hopes of turning it into an antique shop. By the time she had spent $100,000 on renovations, the place looked great but her failing health prevented her from realizing her dream.

James and Barbara Stovall bought the house in 1981, and planned to demolish it and build condominiums. On the eve of destruction, they realized that the charming mansion was too special to be torn down and decided to turn the house into a beautiful restaurant.

In 1987, Italian immigrant Bruno Serato purchased the restaurant and has had two decades of rave reviews. Former U.S. presidents such as Jimmy Carter and, movie stars including Danny DeVito, and other celebrities have enjoyed meals at the Anaheim White House Restaurant. (Pop star Madonna has hired the restaurant to cater for her.)

Though classy and lovely, an undercurrent of unrest runs through the place.

Ghosts keep employees Adam Porter and Marissa Hadley on their toes in this elegant California restaurant. (Leslie Rule)

Did a woman meet her death at the top of these stairs? (Leslie Rule)

John told me about the new waitress he had hired, who quit just days later. He had sent her upstairs on a slow night to polish the glassware. "She came downstairs, hysterical," John confided. "I said, 'Heather, get a hold of yourself.'"

He followed the distraught young woman upstairs where she pointed at the accordion-like room dividers used to section off areas for private parties. Heather had seen the room dividers opening and closing, as if guided by unseen hands.

Who haunts the place? Legend has it that a child of an early resident was hit and killed by a trolley on the road outside. Extensive research, however, has failed to turn up anything to validate the rumor.

"A retired detective was here for dinner one night," John told me. "I offered him a tour and he declined. He told me that he already knew the house well, and that a murder had occurred here."

According to the account, a woman had been home alone in the huge mansion when someone broke in, murdered her, and dragged her to the attic.

John mentioned that the paranormal investigators had captured a ghostly voice on tape, saying, "don't drag me."

My many hours in two different California libraries failed to validate the story. Maybe the detective had been pulling John's leg. Or maybe the murder did happen and had not been reported in the newspapers.

The mansion does not *feel* like a murder occurred there. Those of us who are sensitive often perceive a heaviness in places with violent pasts and come away from the scene feeling sad. The Anaheim White House Restaurant, however, has a light, pleasant ambience. While restless spirits may be present, they likely died more gentle deaths. Perhaps the good doctor is still there, maybe with one of the tots he delivered. Not all survived to adulthood. Ghostly children would certainly feel safe with the kind doctor. He cared about his expectant mothers and their little ones. It did not matter if a patient could not pay. He never turned anyone away. Perhaps it is Dr. Truxaw's shadowy apparition seen in the restaurant hallway. And maybe he is the ghost who peers over workers' shoulders. Employees say they often get the feeling that someone is standing behind them.

Waiter Richard Villa once heard the upstairs room dividers opening and shutting. "It was in the winter around 1:30 a.m.," he told me. "I thought it was a prank. I went downstairs to ask the manager who else was there and he said, 'No one.'"

Waitress Marissa Hadley confessed to something odd that she experienced in a downstairs hallway. She had just put away several tray jacks (the folding stands that support big trays). After she leaned the folded jacks against the wall, she turned away. "I turned back a second later and the stands were out, standing up in the middle of the hallway!"

Waiter Adam Porter said that sometimes, after closing, the staff will hear the distinctive popping sound of the refrigerator opening when there is no one in the kitchen.

It is probably just Dr. Truxaw, looking for a midnight snack.

ANAHEIM WHITE HOUSE RESTAURANT
887 S. Anaheim Boulevard
Anaheim, California 92805
(714) 772-1381
www.anaheimwhitehouse.com

Spotlight on the Investigators

A number of entities may lurk in a Warwick, New York, restaurant, according to the folks at North Jersey Paranormal Research (NJPR). The Italian Villa Restaurant, popular for its fine cuisine and charming ambience, was the focus of an investigation by the NJPR who gathered at the historic structure in October 2005.

"The house was built in the late 1700s for war veteran Levi Ellis," said Mark Johnson, spokesperson for the group. The elegant whitewashed mansion was home to several families, including Harry and Cecelia Emily Vail who moved in around 1920 with their sons, Harry, nineteen, Roy, eighteen, and daughter Emily, thirteen.

A death in the home shocked neighbors in December 1979. An elderly Vail family member died from a self-inflicted gunshot wound in what is today one of the restaurant's main dining rooms. The NJPR team speculates that tragedy may account for much of the activity in the house.

NJPR formed in 2003 and has conducted over fifty investigations. "We currently have seventeen members from all walks of life, including a fire captain, a policeman, an engineer, several computer specialists, business owners, and everyday people looking for answers," said Mark, who stresses that one of their goals is to educate the public about the paranormal.

As the team approached the mansion on the day of the investigation, Gretchen Mendel witnessed an apparition of a little girl in an attic window. They later learned that a girl may have died from an illness while living in the home.

The group captured a number of EVPs in the mansion, including a whispered voice saying, "It's here," and a man's voice in an attic bedroom, saying, "Get out."

While interviewing staff at the Italian Villa Restaurant, NJPR learned of an odd event that happened during a heavy snowstorm. Employees looked out of an upstairs window during the night and noted that two old oak trees had fallen. In the morning they were stunned to find that the trees were still standing. The employees may have witnessed a scene from centuries before, when two other mighty oaks fell.

ITALIAN VILLA RESTAURANT
274 Route 94 S
Warwick, New York 10990
(845) 987-1500

NORTH JERSEY PARANORMAL RESEARCH
www.nnjpr.org

Hungry and Haunted

IN THE NEWS

No Time to Chat

According to Lucia Anderson of the *Free Lance-Star* in Fredericksburg, Virginia, a popular restaurant in the area is home to a restless spirit. In the October 31, 2005, issue of the newspaper she reported an apparition sighting at Smythe's Cottage and Tavern. Customer Paul Ledford was enjoying his meal in the Civil War–era structure when a short, heavy woman in old-time garments bustled past his table. "She was in a hurry. She had a goal," the paper quoted him, and added that she wore a long dark dress and a white apron.

Interestingly, the spirit appeared at the same time a paranormal investigative team was gathering data in another part of the building. The startled diner was not aware of investigators until after his ghost encounter.

Dawn Powell and Patience Trochelman of the Virginia Area Paranormal Onsite Researchers (VAPOR) were disappointed that they did not see the apparition. They did, however, manage to capture unexplained streaking lights on video in the back dining room at the historical site.

Lucia Anderson interviewed the Smythe Cottage owner, Jim Frakes, who is in his element when sharing ghost stories with enthralled customers.

Witnesses have reported activity around the closet in an upstairs room at the cottage, including a closet door opening on its own and a white mist that originates from the closet.

Jim Frakes told the reporter that the ghost also blows out candles and plays with silverware. Legend has it that the spirit belongs to a woman who hanged herself in the stairwell because her husband accused her of sharing secret information with Union soldiers.

SMYTHE'S COTTAGE AND TAVERN
303 Fauquier Street
Fredericksburg, Virginia 22401
(540) 373-1645

FADING AWAY

Chiane's, a downtown Torrington, Connecticut, café is visited by the mysterious presence of a young man, reported Rick Klimanowski of the *Register Citizen*. According to the September 6, 2004, article, the ghostly fellow may be part of a group of spirits attached to the old building.

Diane Persechino was hard at work in Chiane's when she heard conversation floating down from upstairs. She figured that a radio had been left on and went to investigate but the conversation stopped when she reached the top of the stairs.

Diane and others have glimpsed a dark-haired young man with a slender build. "The kid will be there and then he fades," she told the reporter, explaining that he had once disappeared behind a pillar.

The apparition has appeared so solid that staff members have actually spoken to him before realizing he is a ghost. Diane, a reformed skeptic, and her business partner Charlie Marczewski looked for answers at the Torrington Historical Society. They learned that the building was constructed in 1902, and originally owned by George Lilley, who later became governor of Connecticut. The Historical Society offered nothing to explain the root of the haunting.

CHIANE'S GOURMET CAFÉ & COFFEE BAR
77 Main Street
Torrington, Connecticut 06790
(860) 489-0707
www.chianes.com

Adam and Eve

In their July 7, 2006, report, the Norwich, Norfolk's *Evening News 24* featured the haunting of the Adam and Eve Pub. They reported that the city's oldest pub, which has been quenching thirst for under 500 years, has a stubborn spirit who has been around nearly as long.

During a 1549 battle, Lord Sheffield led the king's troops in the area. When Robert Kett and his men confronted him, Sheffield realized that he'd been beaten. In an attempt to spare his life he offered himself as a hostage and removed his helmet, but the plan backfired. A butcher attacked Sheffield with a meat cleaver. The wounded man was carried to Adam and Eve's Pub, where he died on a table.

Soon after, according to the *Evening News*, Lord Sheffield's ghost appeared in the pub and has been manifesting there ever since. Some have spotted the apparition climbing the stairs. The ghost is also blamed for the mysterious disappearance of items. Things vanish from the tables, only to materialize again, days later on the other side of the room.

Adam and Eve
Bishopgate
Norwich, Norfolk
NR3 1R2
Telephone: 01603-667423
www.adamandevenorwich.com

DESPERATE MEASURES

A beautiful ghost named Joesphine haunts the Stottsville Inn, in Pomeroy, Pennsylvania, reported the *ParkesBurg Post Ledger* on December 1, 2005.

Reporter Joe D'Angelo wrote that the haunting may be the result of a murder/suicide believed to have occurred there in the 1800s. A framed copy of a peculiar suicide note is on display at the inn. Horace Chandler, who killed his nineteen-year-old bride, penned a note stating that he planned to go to the barn and bite a cow's leg so that it would kick him in the head and send him to his grave.

Michael Buono Jr., co-owner of the full-service Victorian Bed and Breakfast, led the reporter to room 305, which was the scene of a horrific tragedy. It was there, the innkeeper explained, that Horace had discovered Joesphine with her lover, Chadwin Martin, and in a jealous rage had strangled them both.

A guest spending the night in room 305 awoke at 4:00 a.m. to find Joesphine leaning over the bed. He was so shocked by the encounter that he was unable to go back to sleep.

Folks like to visit the inn and its Busy Bee Pub as much for the cozy ambience as for the opportunity to be spooked. In addition to startling guests with sudden appearances, the ghosts are also blamed for odd scratching sounds, lights going on and off, and doors opening and closing on their own.

STOTTSVILLE INN
3486 Strasburg Road
Pomeroy, Pennsylvania 19367
(610) 857-4090
www.Stottsville.com

A FRIENDLY GHOST

Ladies of the evening from a bygone time have been seen walking through the brick walls at Coyote Joe's Bar and Grill in Prescott, Arizona, reported Lynda Roberts in the March 31, 2006, edition of *Eraunews*. The three-story building housed a brothel and an opium den in the 1800s and employees believe that spirits from that era still remain.

Cooks frequently witness utensils flying from kitchen shelves, and children are treated to candy by a friendly ghost. According to the news account, when kids point at the candy machine they are sometimes surprised to see the candy magically appear before their parents can reach into their pockets for change.

COYOTE JOE'S BAR AND GRILL
214 S. Montezuma Street
Prescott, Arizona 86303
(928) 778-9570
www.coyotejoesgrill.com

MAKING MISCHIEF

According to an October 2007 issue of the *Daily Journal*, a Chicago tavern is haunted by a ghost who keeps the staff on their toes. Columnist Jacquee Thomas wrote that she stopped in each Halloween season for her annual "ghost report."

One bartender, the article revealed, began his career at the pub as a stubborn skeptic. He was not moved by fellow workers' accounts of mysterious footsteps echoing from the pub's second story. He just laughed when they spoke of phantom fingers tapping them on the shoulders, and brazenly announced to the others that he did not believe in ghosts.

The skeptical bartender told Jacquee that shortly after his comment, he became a believer when he felt a distinctive tug on his sweater.

Colin Cordwell, the pub's owner, told the reporter that the mischievous ghost was a mentally challenged girl named Sharon who had once lived on the second floor of the building. He said she was probably responsible for locking patrons in the second-floor ladies' room. In addition, witnesses have seen bar stools inexplicably topple, and a customer had his own drink pushed into his face.

RED LION PUB
2446 N. Lincoln Avenue
Chicago, Illinois 60614
(773) 348-2695

HEARING IS BELIEVING

The *Daily Lobo*, the award-winning student newspaper of the University of New Mexico, covered the strange goings-on at the Church Street Café in Albuquerque's Old Town. The November 14, 2001, article reported that the Mexican restaurant, housed in a 1709 pueblo-style structure, is believed to be haunted by a naughty ghost named Sarah.

A crew from the *Daily Lobo* followed the Southwest Ghost Hunters' Association on their investigation of the café and witnessed an inexplicable knocking on the wall. Four distinctive raps were heard twice.

Marie Coleman, proprietor and owner of the Church Street Café since 1992, said, "When I first bought it, I never believed in ghosts." Her tune changed when she heard disembodied laughter in the empty building. Other paranormal activity includes toilets flushing by themselves, items vanishing without reason, and unseen hands tossing pebbles.

The article noted that the Southwest Ghost Hunters' Association obtained a number of photographs containing orbs, anomalous round spots that appear on film that many believe represent the energy of spirits.

CHURCH STREET CAFÉ
2111 Church Street NW
Albuquerque, New Mexico 87104
(505) 247-8522
www.churchstreetcafe.com

DON'T YOU KNOW?

A bartender and patrons fled from a Scottsdale, Arizona, bar after a ghost swore at them, reported Brian Smith of the *Phoenix New Times*. The April 5, 2001, article described the eerie event that had occurred at the TT Roadhouse in the early afternoon three years earlier.

Four customers and bar manager Lucy Paris were shocked when the jukebox suddenly grew quiet and a raspy, angry voice emanated from the television speakers and called them a vulgar name three times before adding, "Don't you know? Don't you know?"

The stunned group rushed through the front door and huddled in the parking lot, recalled customer John Marinick who told Smith, "It was extraordinary. What is weird was that voice was really, really angry."

Marinick added that they investigated to see if someone had rigged the speakers as a practical joke, but found all the electronics intact.

Employees and customers also told the reporter about empty beer pitchers that flew off the bar, drinks that fell over without cause, and bar stools tossed through the air.

Built as a ranch house in 1953, the structure has served as a bar since 1963 and has seen many drunks come and go—including one who left his glass half full when he went to get something from his car. When he tried to cross Sixty-eighth Street in front of the bar, he was fatally injured by an automobile.

The half-drunken beer was placed on the shelf behind the bar and kept as a memorial for many years until Brad Henrich purchased the business in 1995. He tossed out the old dirty glass before the former owner could tell him of its importance.

The paper noted that the TT Roadhouse is next door to the mortuary and is decorated with gruesome artifacts such as skulls and shrunken heads.

TT ROADHOUSE
2915 N. Sixty-eighth Street
Scottsdale, Arizona 85251
(480) 947-8723

GHOST IN THE
WINDOW

Windows, designed to provide views and to let the sunlight in, are more ubiquitous than mirrors. Most people look *through* them and not *at* them, unless, of course, they are window washers in search of smudges.

Yet, windows are not just transparent sheets of glass. They, too, reflect the world around them *and* sometimes the *other* world beyond. Next time you find yourself in a room brightened with artificial light as the hands of the clock point to the p.m., stop for a moment and gaze at the window. You will see your reflection, for with the black of night pressing against it, the window becomes a mirror. The effect is reversed in the daylight. Windows in dimly lit rooms, viewed from outside (especially from a distance), turn to black, blank squares, and the stage is set for strangers from the Other Side to manifest.

While it is probable that ghosts in windows are seen more frequently when the glass is in reflective mode, sightings are reported in all types of conditions at all times of the day and night. Indeed, the number of sightings rank right up there with apparitions in the mirror.

As my mother mentioned in the foreword of this book, she and I shared a startling sighting of a ghost in the window. It was 1975 when we checked the mailbox at my sister's former residence on 160th Street near Tukwilla, Washington. I will never forget the angry, apelike face that glared at us, our simultaneous gasps, and the way the car lurched forward as my mother quickly pressed her foot to the gas pedal. It did not occur to me that we had seen a ghost until my mother mentioned it later that day. It was not the first or the last time that she would suggest that an odd sighting with a seemingly normal human being was actually a ghost encounter.

Most of these experiences occurred when I was a teenager or in my early twenties. That was a time, however, when I dismissed my mother's opinions as fanciful notions or ridiculous out-of-date observations.

Now, with a decade of ghost research behind me and my once-fresh eyes peering from bifocal lenses, my mother does not seem quite as out of touch as she once did. In fact, I wonder now why I doubted our ghost in the window encounter—especially since it was not the first time that I had seen something in the window of that house.

Months before the day we were frightened by the enraged face, I had been staying with my sister in the old, white house. While she was at work, I walked to the store. When I returned, I stepped onto the path to the front door, glanced at the picture window, and froze. I saw three figures in the living room. I was not close enough to register details, yet I saw that one was a woman and that the other two were men. They were not looking out of the window or standing directly in front of it. They stood several feet from each other in the middle of the room, as if they were engaged in a conversation.

I took all of this in instantly as a sudden shock rocked me. I wish now that I had been more curious and less afraid. I wish I had stared at the scene and soaked up the details. Instead, I hurried to the landlord's house next door and called my father and asked him to come get me.

I still shiver when I remember that house. It was always cold. We stood as close to the old heater as we could get, desperate to get warm—but it never quite happened.

We were afraid there. We sensed the ghosts. We did not, however, realize that we were dealing with anything out of the ordinary. As readers of my earlier books might remember, I grew up in a haunted house and thought that all houses came with spirits. In my childhood home, I heard rather than saw things.

Seeing ghosts was a new experience for me, and I will never forget my two sightings that year. Now, as a paranormal researcher, I have witnessed very few inexplicable things, despite the fact I have been to hundreds of haunted places. I have interviewed many people who have seen apparitions, and a number of them involved windows.

The following are a few cases of ghosts seen in windows.

PEERING SPINSTER

Folks are sometimes startled by a pale face peering from the window of one of the most famous houses in Massachusetts. The House of the Seven Gables in Salem is thought by many to be the inspiration for Nathaniel Hawthorne's novel *The House of the Seven Gables*. The spooky black house with craggy trees poking up around it is the oldest surviving wooden mansion in New England. The house, built in 1668, was once home to Hawthorne's spinster cousin Susannah Ingersoll.

Many believe it is her ghost who rattles about the house, which is now a museum, and watches from an upstairs window.

HOUSE OF THE SEVEN GABLES AKA TURNER-INGERSOLL MANSION
54 Turner Street
Salem, Massachusetts 01970
www.7gables.org

What restless spirit wanders the House of the Seven Gables? (Leslie Rule)

KEMPER GHOST

Local lore says that a trapped spirit resides in a lovely mansion on Lake Michigan beside Kenosha County Park in Kenosha, Wisconsin. The 1860s structure was home to Wisconsin's first senator, Charles Durkee. Later, it was known as Kemper Hall and served as an Episcopal girls' school for over a century, finally closing its doors in 1975.

Many claim that they have seen the apparition of a woman framed in an upstairs window. She is believed to be a nun who mysteriously vanished during her stay at the school around the turn of the nineteenth century.

The building, now known as Kemper Hall, is used for a variety of special events.

KEMPER HALL
6501 Third Avenue
Kenosha, Wisconsin 53143

KANSAS CITY CASTLE

An apparition has been seen in the window of the Writers Place, a Kansas City, Missouri, literary center. The castlelike structure in the Valentine neighborhood is home to a nonprofit group that promotes and nurtures writers. The organization shares the space with publisher Helicon Nine, who occupies the third floor.

Built in 1909 as a private residence, the castle has also served as a brothel, an apartment house, and a church. One evening in 1998, Bob Stewart, former president of the board, pulled into the driveway

The Kansas City castle is a favorite place for writers (and ghosts) to gather. (Leslie Rule)

one evening and saw someone walking past an upstairs office window. He soon discovered, however, that the place was locked up, the burglar alarm was turned on, and no one else was there.

On a separate occasion, a witness was heading up the stairs when she glimpsed the silhouette of a woman with long hair and a long skirt. The figure glided past an upstairs window and dissolved. Others have seen a similar figure on a second-floor balcony. And a former board officer once saw the ghost of a man in a tuxedo at the foot of the staircase. Witnesses have also heard phantom footsteps on the stairs, and smelled perfume, cologne, and other "weird smells."

A mysterious figure has been seen in the upstairs window of the Writers Place. (Leslie Rule)

A tiny dog named Tootie was keeping her owner company in the mansion when she suddenly disappeared. She was soon discovered, unharmed, in the big, empty claw-foot bathtub. A writer who had helped search for her said that "there was no way she could have gotten in there by herself."

THE WRITERS PLACE
3607 Pennsylvania
Kansas City, Missouri 64111
(816) 753-1090
www.writersplace.org

MONTEZUMA GHOST

Neighbors report seeing the face of a long dead occupant in the tower window of an 1887 mansion in San Diego, California. The Villa Montezuma was once the site of séances, hosted by the original owner Jesse Shepard—a musician and "spiritualist" who tried to channel the ghosts of musicians.

Today, the magnificent mansion is a museum, run by the San Diego Historical Society. Apparently, Jesse's ghost has joined those he once attempted to communicate with.

VILLA MONTEZUMA
1925 K Street
San Diego, California 92102
(610) 232-6203

7
Business
as Usual

Whether they toil forty hours a week or work part-time shifts, most folks feel a connection with their places of employment. Many dedicated employees have died—only to return to work. Perhaps they left some unfinished business there, or maybe they just don't realize that they are dead.

Whatever the reason, earthbound spirits in the workplace are not uncommon. Here are a few cases.

Where Ghosts Play

Ghosts at a costume shop in Scottdale, Pennsylvania, sometimes make their presence known through a mirror. They do not, however, *appear* in the mirror: They remove it from the wall.

Brian Corcoran of Vintage Costumes LLC told me that a number of spirits roam the grounds of his 1860s estate where a former carriage house serves as the costume shop.

After the mirror repeatedly and mysteriously popped off of the wall in a second-floor room of the fifteen-room brick mansion, it was finally moved to another part of the home and has stayed put ever since.

The problem started when the mirror somehow disengaged itself from the wall and fell unbroken to the floor. Sometime later, Brian awoke in the night to a tremendous crash only to find that the mirror had flown off of the wall and landed on the floor without suffering so much as a crack. He glanced at the clock and noted the time. It was a little past 2:00 a.m. The next day he discovered that a pal had also awakened at the exact moment. They soon learned that a mutual friend had died in the hospital at that precise time.

"My friend was a prankster," said Brian, who thinks that the departed was playing one last joke. While his friend may have moved on, other spirits remain.

A costume shop with a booming Halloween business is a fitting place for ghosts to play and the very people who inspired the venture may be haunting the place—*Brian's ancestors.*

Seven generations of Brian's family have lived on the property, some leaving souvenirs behind. A few years back, Brian opened a dusty, old trunk in the attic and discovered the clothing of his great-grandparents. He figured that the vintage frocks and period jackets would make unique Halloween costumes so he set up shop and rented them out. When the merchandise was snatched up, Brian and his partner, Ruth Peterson, went into business. Today they supply garments for plays, films, and costume parties. "Halloween is our big season," said Brian, who designs and sews along with Ruth and three hired seamstresses. "Orders start coming in in June."

Although folks visit the huge barnlike shop beside the mansion on the hill to pick out costumes to rent or buy, some of his customers are spooked. Visitors have seen doors open and shut on their own and have heard the ghostly giggles of phantom children.

Items in the place often mysteriously vanish, only to turn up again in unexpected spots. The strong, flowery perfume of an unseen lady permeates the air, and sudden, icy gusts announce another presence.

Brian recalled an odd encounter early on a frosty winter morning in the 1970s, when he walked his sheepdog, Mickey, across the seventy-five acre estate. He glanced up to see an old man in a black suit on a hilltop at the edge of the woods. He was about thirty feet away, close enough for Brian to notice his pale skin and expressionless features.

"Can I help you?" Brian asked, startled to discover a trespasser. "I was about to tell him that he was on private property when he turned and walked into the woods."

Brian hurried after him, following him through the trees and calling out to him. "I couldn't catch up to him," he remembered. Brian was young and agile and should have been able to overtake the old gentleman. Yet, no matter how fast he ran, the stranger managed to maintain the distance between them.

"It was rugged," he said. "I had to walk around fallen limbs and step over brush." The trespasser seemed unhindered, never stooping or faltering. Occasionally, he would disappear behind a tree and then emerge again.

Brian followed the man to the clearing, stepped out of the woods, and looked around, but the old fellow was gone.

As he stood there shivering in the cold, white light of winter, Brian's gaze went to the graveyard. It was as if the trespasser had led him there. He was familiar with the gray, weathered tombstones, overgrown with weeds. The cemetery was no longer tended. Those who rested there had died in the 1800s and had no surviving loved ones left to care for the graves.

"There are about fifteen graves there," said Brian, adding that he assumes some belong to his ancestors.

Where did the old man go? Brian searched but could not find him. His hasty disappearance made no sense. But nothing about the encounter made sense. Though he had followed the stranger, the brush was not trampled. And the man had made no noise. There had been no sound of twigs snapping underfoot.

While Brian and his dog sent little puffs of steam from their mouths each time they exhaled into the chill air, the man had not. The detail had registered when Brian first saw him on the hill. Maybe the stranger had been holding his breath.

Or maybe, he had no breath.

Maybe he had been laid out in his Sunday best a century before in the parlor of the mansion as visitors came for one last look. Maybe he was the poor man who had dropped dead when the home had served as the town's post office and general store.

Maybe he was the Whistler.

Every so often over the years, someone in the family would hear him. "It was always right before a family member died," said Brian, who heard the eerie whistling in the mansion at the same moment that his uncle passed away in a distant hospital.

The unnatural events don't frighten Brian. The spooky ambience is an inspiration for his creativity. In addition to producing costumes, he also designs and assembles scary sets for Halloween parties. Sometimes when visitors look over his collection of creepy props, they pause to scrutinize a skeleton, marveling at its realistic appearance.

The skeleton *is* real. Brian inherited it along with his mother's antique tea set and a number of other relics. When his mother was a young woman, she saw it in a doctor's office and was intrigued. "The doctor went to medical school in England," he said, explaining that students obtained unidentified bodies from the morgue and dissected them as part of their training. The skeleton had once been a young woman, fished out of the Thames River in London sometime around the turn of the nineteenth century. A crack in the middle of her forehead indicates that she may have been a victim of violence.

The doctor eventually gave the skeleton to Brian's mother, who named her Sheba. The skeleton has been around as long as he can remember, though she was usually stashed in a closet. Sometimes, when he was a youngster, the grinning, bony figure would startle him but he is used to her now.

Perhaps the poor lady is responsible for some of the paranormal activity in the place. Researchers have noted a strong link between ghosts and their remains. If indeed the London lady's spirit is still around, she may be fascinated with Brian's creations. Some of his costumes look as if they come right out of nineteenth-century London. Perhaps she recognizes the clothing she wore in happier times, before she was so carelessly tossed into the Thames.

Perhaps it is she who dabs on the flowery perfume and prances about the place, entertaining the giggling ghostly children.

VINTAGE COSTUMES LLC
990 Scottdale Dawson Road
Scottdale, Pennsylvania 15683
(724) 887-8255

YBOR CITY

"Is anybody here with us?" asked Shaun Jones as she held a tape recorder out to the huge, dark room on the second floor of the old cigar factory.

It was a typical muggy autumn evening in Ybor City, Florida, and the founder and director of the Florida Ghost Team did not have to wait long for a response from whatever lurked in the big, barnlike building.

"We heard a loud bang and then what sounded like something heavy being dragged across the wooden floor," she said. Team member Amanda Haines stood beside her and both women turned on their flashlights, shooting beams of light in the direction of the noise. They were alone. The dozens of other folks who had gathered for the investigation had gone outside for a break from the stifling, hot, dusty space.

"We turned our flashlights off and asked, 'Who is here with us?'" Shaun told me. "We heard something about ten feet away. It sounded like a loud click."

As the two wandered through the factory, they heard the sound of footsteps, echoing from the third floor. Although they were positive that everyone else was outside, they went upstairs just to be sure. They checked every nook and cranny and confirmed that no other live human being was present. The group, formed in 2003, has conducted approximately 250 investigations. Their inspections are thorough and data is carefully recorded, leaving no room for error.

"We decided to go outside to get some air," Shaun said. "With no electricity, it was extremely hot in the factory. As we walked down the stairs, we heard footsteps running up behind us."

The women whirled around, but once again there was no one there.

❧

Spanish-born Vicente Martinez Ybor founded Ybor City in 1886 as a center for cigar manufacturing. When he first set foot there it was a mosquito-infested swamp where alligators roamed. As he established the first cigar factory, droves of immigrants arrived to work in it. Spaniards, Cubans, Italians, Germans, and Jews were among those who made the place their home.

Ybor City (actually a section of Tampa) soon earned Tampa the nickname of "Cigar Capital of the World" as its two-hundred-plus factories produced millions of cigars.

Today Ybor City is a National Historic District and a popular tourist attraction. Inlaid brick paths weave past the old cigar factories that now house some of the sixty bars and restaurants that nourish the crowds.

I visited Ybor City to meet with Shaun Jones and the Florida Ghost Team on a rainy afternoon in October 2007. We met at the old factory, once known as the Oliva Tobacco Company, hours before Shaun and Amanda's encounter with the unseen presence.

Shaun introduced me to Joann Almeida who took me through the big building. It was the last known cigar factory made of wood in existence. The three

James Emory has encountered entities inside of the Oliva Tobacco Company in Ybor City. (Leslie Rule)

stories of 30,000 square feet had recently been cleared of debris by an ambitious group of young people.

Blake and James Emory, two brothers in their early twenties, had made the huge, whitewashed factory their home and business for the past year. They were creative souls who had turned the place into an art mecca. The Emorys and a few of their friends had put on plays there and were in the process of setting up an art gallery when they heard discouraging news. Despite the agreement he had made with

Joann Almeida sits near the spot where she once witnessed a ghost in an old cigar factory. (Leslie Rule)

them, the building's owner was now finagling a deal. The historic factory would be sold soon and a hotel would occupy the space.

"They are disappointed," Joann told me as I followed her up the flight of wooden steps to the sweltering third floor. "They worked really hard on this place."

Unfinished art projects sat amongst the dusty artifacts of yesteryear. "You should have seen it before they cleared it out," she said. "It was stacked to the ceiling with junk."

Joann paused beside an upstairs window and said, "Blake saw an apparition here. It looked like a man in a hat and he walked by quickly."

She had also seen a ghost in the building and she showed me where the fleeting, shadowy figure had crossed the room on the second floor.

The Emorys were spooked, but not by the apparitions. They were disturbed by the ghostly voices they heard when they had spent the night in sleeping bags on the first floor. They awoke to the sounds of what sounded like babbling in a foreign tongue.

A visitor once left the place, terrified, after he ducked into the nonfunctioning, windowless, ground-level bathroom to look around. "He shut the door," Joann said. "But when he tried to leave, he couldn't get the door open. It was as if someone was putting pressure on the door from the outside. He thought that someone was playing a prank on him."

In this case, the prankster was not a live human being.

On another occasion, friends of James expressed an interest in the ghosts and someone suggested a séance. A few of the Emorys' friends gathered on the second floor. When they sat down in the dark on the wooden floor for an impromptu séance, they suddenly heard glass shattering. After they turned the light back on, they found that the

Though they died decades ago, some of those who once toiled in the Oliva Tobacco Company are still hard at work. (Leslie Rule)

The Florida Ghost Team poses with a statue of the Ybor City founder shortly before their investigation of a haunted cigar factory. Back row, left to right: Wendy Spiller, Amanda Haines. Front row, left to right: Shawn Porter, Shaun Jones, Kevin O'Connor, Trevor Fitch. (Leslie Rule)

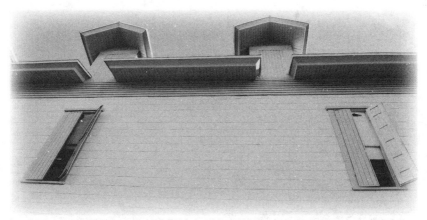

Investigators detected paranormal activity within the walls of this old factory. (Leslie Rule)

floor was littered with shards of glass. "We had no idea where the glass came from," James told me.

Who are the ghosts of the old factory?

"The workers would chew tobacco and spit on the floor," James said. "The place was unsanitary and many of them got tuberculosis. The disease was rampant in the area. A lot of people died from it."

James had researched the history of the building and found another possible source for the haunting. "It was once used as a morgue," he said, adding that he was unable to find details.

Days after their investigation, the Florida Ghost Team listened to the audiotapes they recorded that night and heard something interesting.

The ghostly response came right after Shaun Jones asked the empty room, "Who is here with us?"

The answer was simple. The tape-recorded female voice replied, "Me."

AFTER HOURS

A mysterious spirit haunts an Ohio grocery store. I recently received a letter from Christine Davis, who worked as a cashier at the store in the spring of 2006 when she encountered the apparition.

Here is an excerpt from her letter:

I worked at a Miller's New Market, a small grocery store in Genoa, Ohio, where my mom is the second shift manager. The store stays open until midnight, and I often worked the late shift with my mom. One night, it was just the two of us working. I was at the cash register and my mom was doing paperwork in the office.

It was a slow night, with just a couple of customers coming in during the last hour. Around 11:45 p.m., I heard a noise that sounded like something was knocked off of a shelf. The noise wasn't unusual. I figured a customer must have slipped in when I wasn't paying attention.

Shortly after, I heard what sounded like the heel of a shoe squeaking on the floor. When the clock hit midnight, my mom went to lock the entrance doors. That was normally the time that I pulled my register drawer to take to the office for the deposit. But I told my mom that there was someone still in the store, so we stood there and waited. After a few moments, my mom asked me if I was sure that someone was in the store.

I told her that I was sure I had heard someone. She made an announcement over the speaker system, saying that the store was closed and that all customers should bring their purchases to the checkout line. Nobody came.

My mom looked at me like I was nuts, but I insisted that someone was in the store with us. I walked around and looked down the aisles. Then I heard the distinctive sound of a freezer door shutting. I walked back to the frozen food section but still could not find anyone.

I was starting to get irritated, because I knew someone was there, but could not find them. I looked down every aisle. Then I searched the stock room, break room, bakery, and the restrooms. I was kind of wondering if I was going crazy as I walked back to the front of the store and admitted to my mom that I was wrong. All the customers had left.

I pulled my register drawer and we went to the cashier's office. Ten minutes later, I headed toward the back of the store so I could clock us out. Afterward, I headed back to the front, walking through the produce section and around to the deli area. I looked up and saw a person by the deli case. I stopped dead in my tracks and froze.

I saw her profile for a split second, but it was long enough to see that she was wearing jeans, a long-sleeved white shirt, and a royal blue apron or smock. She was thin with brown hair that fell just past her shoulders.

I felt like I was rooted to the spot for an eternity. I then ran up to the front where my mom was waiting. She joked, "You look like you've just seen a ghost."

"I did!" I said.

Her eyes got real big and she said, "Oh my God, you saw the ghost?"

I said, "What do you mean 'the ghost'"? She told me that the ghost had been seen by a couple of employees. That was probably the strangest, scariest situation I had ever been in. I was shaking the whole drive back to my house.

Genoa is a small, quiet town. It is possible that someone who worked at Miller's is now dead, but I don't think anyone died in that store.

Christine and I corresponded, as we both researched to try to discover the identity of the ghost. So far, all we know is that an employee named Donna died of cancer. But we don't know what she looked like or when she died.

We also learned that Latham's Grocery Store once had occupied the building. And word has it that their employees wore royal blue smocks, like the one the apparition wore. Since employees are not allowed to wear jeans now, Christine believes the woman may have been from an earlier era.

When Christine's mom called the store manager to ask if I could mention the store in the book, he not only said yes, he extended an invitation for me to spend the night in the store! Unfortunately, my ghost travels were already booked and did not take me near Ohio.

Beyond the Misty Horizon

In June 2006, a ghost aboard an old whaling ship moored in Mystic Seaport in Mystic, Connecticut, drew the attention of paranormal investigators according to a number of newspaper reports, including the *Boston Globe*.

An apparition was seen by three people on separate occasions on the SS *Charles W. Morgan*, the oldest square-rigged merchant vessel in existence. Witnesses contacted the Rhode Island Paranormal Research Group, and sparked the interest of the team's director, Andrew Laird.

Everyone described the ghost as a man in dated clothing who smoked a pipe and sat atop a pile of rope. The encounters occurred below deck, in the area once used to strip blubber from whales.

The figure appeared so solid that he was sometimes mistaken for an actor, hired to add flavor to the ambience. The ghost researchers were so intrigued by the sightings that they sought and were granted permission by the Museum of America and the Sea, curators of the *Morgan*, to conduct a formal investigation. The team assembled on a rainy Saturday night in June armed with equipment that included electromagnetic field detectors to measure energy fields and digital recorders to capture phantom voices. Though the group included psychics, it was the team director who actually *saw* a ghost. Andrew Laird had seen an apparition just once before in two decades as a paranormal researcher.

At first Andrew did not realize that the man he saw on deck was not of flesh and blood. The apparition ignored an attempt at conversation and stepped behind a mast and vanished.

The *Charles W. Morgan*, built of live oak and launched in 1841, has sailed through rough waters and seen much death. The ghost, however, may be someone attached to the vessel simply because it had meant so much to him in life. My archive research turned up a 1918 article in the *New Oxford Item* with the headline, "Finds Wealth in Dream Ship. Aged Skipper Brings Home Fortune in Boat of Boyhood Fancy."

The article described how Captain Benjamin Cleveland had daydreamed about the *Morgan* as a boy in New Bedford, Massachusetts, and had watched the ship "leave port and sail beyond the misty horizon."

Decades later, at age seventy, when Captain Cleveland learned that the seventy-five-year-old ship was "doomed to the scrap heap," he came out of retirement to purchase the vessel, hired a crew of thirty men, and then got rich whaling. He set records, and newspapers noted that he had the "two largest catches of oil ever brought into New Bedford."

The captain died at his home in New Bedford at eighty-one on June 21, 1925.

A leading theory among paranormal researchers says that some spirits remain earthbound because of a sentimental attachment to a place, person, or thing.

The spirit could also be one of a number of other men who died while working on the ship. In his book, *The Charles W. Morgan*, the late author John F. Leavitt chronicled the life of the vessel, referencing archived ship logs to provide much of the information, including many fatalities.

One death was particularly shocking and unnecessary. It occurred in 1845, during an era when it was legal to flog and shackle shipmates who misbehaved. The whippings were at times so severe that men carried the scars to their graves.

Captain John Sampson had strict rules, which prohibited both card playing and fighting. In June 1845, as the vessel sailed east across the Indian Ocean, two men got in a fight.

The intolerant Captain Sampson ordered a horrific punishment. As the rest of the crew watched, the men were flogged twelve times each and then tossed into the ocean and left to drown in the ship's indifferent wake.

The fact that ghost investigator Andrew Laird spotted the apparition during the month of June suggests that the ghost may be connected to the double killing. A strong correlation between manifestations and anniversaries has been noted by paranormal researchers, and unjust death is frequently tied to hauntings.

When it comes to identifying the ghosts of the *Charles W. Morgan*, however, we have a selection to choose from as numerous fatalities occurred on the ship, including the heartbreaking death of Captain Thomas C. Landers's son Arthur, sixteen, who fell overboard on a July day in 1864.

Other deaths include seventeen-year-old Earl Russel who died of typhoid fever on November 28, 1883, and was buried at sea.

The crew was horrified to see one of their whale boats lost to their wounded prey in 1894. The six-man boat of hunters was no match for the big bull sperm whale who reacted violently when harpooned. The injured beast exploded into a rage. Whipped into a frenzy, the whale thrashed against the boat, throwing its occupants into the sea, and turning the vessel into driftwood.

Five survived, but first mate Frederick Swain was killed on impact. His hat bobbed on the waves as he was swallowed by the sea.

In 1921, with eight decades behind her, the *Charles W. Morgan* finished her last voyage when electricity became commonplace and oil was no longer in demand.

Artists and visionaries recognized the beauty of the obsolete vessel. As movie directors cast her in their romantic seafaring films, others rallied to preserve the ship as a museum. Today she is open to the public.

MYSTIC SEAPORT
75 Greenmanville Avenue
Mystic, Connecticut 06355
(860) 572-5315
www.mysticseaport.org

Ghosts at Work

IN THE NEWS

The Night Shift

At the Sam Levitz Furniture Store in Tucson, Arizona, a dedicated employee works overtime yet has not received a paycheck in six years.

According to the *Arizona Daily Wildcat*, workers in the warehouse have seen the man who died on the job in the early morning hours. He materializes around 4:00 a.m. to 5:00 a.m. in the place where he lost his life. He was trying to retrieve a mirror from a high rack but lost his balance and fell. He landed on his back and died on the spot.

Tommy Guerrero, the head security guard in the store, told reporter Katy Graham that he had been aware of the ghostly presence for years.

Michael Greg, another security guard, was quoted saying, "I've come in in the mornings and seen furniture off the racks and on the ground, like somebody pushed it off the top rack in the middle of the night."

In addition to "helping" move the furniture, witnesses, who were alone in the building, have heard the distinctive sound of footsteps.

Staff has surmised that the spirit believes he is still at work and may not realize that his shift is long over.

SAM LEVITZ FURNITURE STORE
3430 E. Thirty-sixth Street
Tucson, Arizona 85713

RUDE CUSTOMER

A bakery in a Sainbury's supermarket in Welwyn Garden City, Hertfordshire, England, has staff thoroughly spooked according to the October 4, 2006, edition of the *Welwyn and Hatfield Times*.

Employees told reporter, Steve Creswell, that paranormal activity at the business has been noted since 2001 but has increased throughout 2006.

Anne Coleman was at work around 6:00 a.m. when she noticed someone walking through the bakery and called out a greeting. When there was no reply, she at first dismissed it as rudeness, until she realized she had seen a ghost. She also confided that she has felt something tug at her feet when she is walking, as if unseen hands are trying to trip her.

The same day that the apparition was spotted, employee John Curry found water pouring from the faucets, the sink full, and the floor flooded. In addition, two of the ovens had been turned on high. Management thoroughly inspected the equipment and could find no logical explanation.

SAINBURY'S
Welwyn Garden City
Hertfordshire, England

SEEING THE DEAD

I wish I could jump into a medium's head and see ghosts through their eyes. For there are those among us who claim to see spirits as vivid and solid looking as live human beings. They have long conversations with spirits, who speak as clearly as you or I. The apparitions are so lifelike that moments may pass before the psychic realizes that they are visiting with a ghost.

For us regular folks, ghost encounters are typically fleeting and vague. Apparitions are usually gone before we can blink, or they appear as shadowy forms. While there *are* cases of everyday people having conversations with lifelike ghosts, these occurrences are rare to the individual, and uncommon among the population.

A few people among us possess amazing clarity of vision. Four of them are featured here. Nancy, Skip, Sharon, and Donna have each impressed me, telling me things that they cannot possibly know—unless they are scrutinizing me through their third eyes.

They can foresee the future and communicate with the dead. They may not *always* be right, but they are accurate so much of the time that they trust their own intuition.

Here is a peek at the lives of those who see the dead.

NANCY

As Nancy Myer glanced up at the top of the staircase in the historic Pittsburgh, Pennsylvania, mansion, she was only a little surprised to see a young woman looking down at her. The woman was "very pregnant," wore a Victorian dress, and dabbed at her eyes with a large handkerchief. The distraught lady was a ghost.

Steve Czetli, Nancy's former husband, snapped a photo of Nancy at that moment. "He took a picture of me in the mirror," said Nancy. "You can see that I am looking up in the photograph. I was looking at the ghost."

Though Steve did not see the apparition, his camera recorded an odd, cloudy thing. "If you look at it closely, you can see her," Nancy said. The entire image is a reflection in an ornately framed mirror, and a grayish, cauliflower-shaped mass seems to be sprouting wispy tendrils. It is, Nancy explained, ectoplasm in the process of forming into a spirit. I studied the photo for a long time, and as I did, the shape of a woman seemed to emerge. Was I really looking at a photograph of a ghost, or was this like picking an image from a cloud? I cannot say for certain, though the weird mass in itself is interesting.

I will let readers study the photo and decide for themselves.

I met Nancy in the early 1990s when my editors at *Woman's World* magazine assigned me an article on psychics who work with police.

The Pennsylvania psychic has worked on hundreds of crime cases and estimates that she has contributed useful information in over 90 percent of them. As directed by the magazine editors, I interviewed a detective who vouched for her.

Psychic Nancy Myer was visiting a haunted mansion when a photographer captured an odd image in the mirror. (Steve Czetli)

Nancy "read" some of the photographs for my first ghost book, *Coast to Coast Ghosts,* and was startlingly accurate. As a result, I trust her ability. And I listened intently as she told me about her encounter with the pregnant Pittsburgh ghost.

The owners of the private residence had hired Nancy to help them. The paranormal activity had escalated, and when a marble fireplace mantle suddenly cracked, they called for psychic intervention. "The owners of the home were arguing," she explained. "The mantle cracked and a shard of marble shot across the room and hit the man in the face."

The spirits in the home were restless, and the psychic soon learned why.

As she studied the apparition on the staircase, she could see that the woman was upset. "She had the most beautiful, porcelain skin," remembered Nancy. "Her hair was pulled back into a bun. She looked like she was due any moment."

"Those men are destroying the peace in my home," the ghost complained to Nancy, who next encountered the spirit of the pregnant woman's husband. It was he, she said, who was causing the commotion.

The mansion's tenants had found windows inexplicably opened on bitterly cold winter days, and items carelessly tossed about. The residents had also been disturbed by the puzzling sound of loud "booms," that seemed to emanate from within the home.

The disgruntled ghosts were trying to drive the residents from the home.

The spirits, Nancy told me, belonged to people who had lived in the house over a century ago. "They had no idea that they were ghosts," she said, explaining that the man's first wife had died during childbirth and he was worried that the constant arguing of the tenants would traumatize his young wife and create complications in her pregnancy.

The ghosts wanted the tenants to leave. When Nancy shared this information with the bickering residents, they vowed to stop fighting.

Over a decade has passed since the psychic investigated the haunted mansion. She has not heard from the tenants and can only assume that the dead and the living have learned to exist in harmony.

SKIP AND SHARON

When nature calls in the middle of the night, most folks have an uneventful trip to the bathroom. But Skip Leingang sometimes finds strangers waiting for him as he walks past his living room.

"The first thing I ask myself is, 'Ghost or burglar?'" Skip told me. For the trespassers appear so solid and lifelike that he cannot determine whether they are flesh and blood until he speaks with them.

The psychic once got up in the night and found a diminutive, dapper gentleman politely perched on a chair. He wore a suit and bow tie and introduced himself as Mr. Peabody. "I didn't want to disturb you so I waited for you to wake up," he said.

Not all lost souls are as courteous. Some, said Skip, burst right into the bedroom and hover over his sleeping form. Mr. Peabody, however, patiently waited.

"I don't know what to do," said the mild-mannered ghost.

"Go to the white light," Skip told him.

"I saw the light, but I didn't know what it was," Mr. Peabody replied before embarking upon his journey. The meek little soul was just one of many spirits who Skip has sent toward the white light, he told me.

Sharon and Skip Leingang can converse with the dead. (Leslie Rule)

While he can see and hear spirits as clearly as if they are live human beings, his wife Sharon usually does not see the dead with her eyes or hear them speak with her ears. Yet she *knows* when they are present, and she senses what they want. "It's a knowing," she told me. "I can't tell you how I know. I just know."

I first met the husband and wife team of psychics when they performed near their home in Federal Way, Washington, in the winter of 2003. A crowd of about sixty sat riveted on folding metal chairs as the charismatic, middle-aged couple stood at the front of the room. One by one, the deceased relatives of those attending made themselves known. The couple took turns relaying the messages from the spirits that the rest of us could not hear or see. Sometimes the psychics mentioned a first name or initials. And sometimes they came up with specific information.

One big, burly guy had tears streaming down his cheeks as Skip gave a detailed description of his dead brother who had popped in to say hi.

About twenty minutes into the group reading, Skip said, "I hear waves over here and I smell saltwater." He pointed at me.

I nodded, acknowledging that his vision made sense. I grew up in Des Moines, Washington, in a house on a hill above the beach. On windy days the waves splattered our windows, leaving traces of salt behind.

"There is someone here who says that his spirit was in your home and that you whispered to him when you were a little girl."

A prickle went up my neck as I shook my head in confusion. I was bewildered, but not because I did not recognize what he was telling me. I knew exactly what he was talking about. Yet, I was so stunned that I could not acknowledge it.

Skip was persistent. "He said you *know* who he is."

I did.

Reverend William John Rule was my father's grandfather. Unlike my father's *father*, John Rule, who terrified us with his horrible temper and mean streak, my great-grandfather was a kind and gentle man and the one positive influence in my father's life when he was a boy.

The Methodist minister was a circuit rider as a young man. This meant he rode his horse throughout the state of Washington and

preached to a number of communities. I had never met him for he died before I was born, but I had heard my parents talking about him many times as a child. They enjoyed telling company that his ghost haunted our house. Our home had been in my family for decades and my great-grandfather had once lived there.

It was common knowledge that our house was haunted, and I wrote about some of the events in an earlier book, *Coast to Coast Ghosts*. But this is the first time I have written about my

The Rule family was happy to share their home with the benign spirit of this man. (author's collection)

great-grandfather's spirit *and* the fact that I whispered to him when I was a child.

When I was about seven years old, I thought I had it all figured out. I told my friends that our house was haunted by a number of ghosts. Some were bad, I'd say, but my great-grandfather was good and he protected us from the evil. I don't remember how I came to that conclusion. Perhaps it was just a childish way of making sense of a home that emanated weird sounds and a dark, creepy feeling. Or perhaps I really was tuning into the reality of the situation.

In my young mind, my great-grandfather had a direct line to God. He was, after all, a minister. My family attended the church where he had once preached. And now that he was in spirit form himself, I figured that he had one foot in heaven. When I didn't want to bother God with a prayer, I talked to my great-grandfather.

I never told a soul that I whispered to him. And I took for granted that he could hear me. He had loved my father, and I was certain that he loved me. I felt safe when I talked to him.

When Skip psychically smelled the saltwater and heard the waves smashing on the beach, he was sensing the thing that had drawn my great-grandfather to Des Moines. He was born in Cornwall, England, and had traveled to the United States in the late 1800s. Although he had lived in a number of places, when he saw the beach in Des Moines, it reminded him of his home in Cornwall and he finally settled there. He raised two sons in the little town on Puget Sound with its craggy cliffs and miles of rocky beach.

I was shocked when Skip reminded me about the whispering. I had not thought of it for years. But Skip was not done. He saw someone else, he told me. "He was walking on the sand and suddenly, he just fell over flat on his back. Do you know who that is?"

No. That was definitely not familiar.

And Sharon, too, was picking up on something. She sensed a grandmotherly figure and the letter "S." That was easy: It was my Grandma Sophie, my mom's mom. We had been very close.

"There is a red square of fabric," Sharon said. "She's showing me this. She drew a picture in the air, of a square about two feet by two feet."

"I don't know what that means," I said.

Sharon was not dissuaded. She told me to ask others in my family, so I phoned my mom the next day and described Sharon's vision.

"Oh!" my mom cried. "That red blanket was *very* significant. We'd had it since I was a little girl, and over the years, it got smaller and smaller."

Grandma had cut away the frayed edges until all that was left was the small square that Sharon described.

The person who fell in the sand? It was my father's father, John Rule, my mother said. He was walking along the beach in San Diego when he had a stroke and fell flat on his back. It was not a fatal incident and I did not remember it.

Had the psychics really been in contact with the ghosts of my grandparents, or were they just reading my mind? They *couldn't* have been reading my mind. For I had not known about my grandma's red blanket or my grandfather's fall.

I believe that Sharon and Skip were getting the information directly from my dead relatives.

While Sharon has always been psychic, Skip developed his ability after a motorcycle accident when he was a young man in the 1970s. The head injury somehow changed his brain, enabling him to see and hear spirits. Others have also experienced this phenomenon. Some cases tell of people who become suddenly psychic after being struck by lightning.

REV. W. J. RULE, 1896

The author's great-grandfather, Reverend William John Rule, traveled by horseback to preach. Though he died before Leslie was born, she feels she knows him well. (author's collection)

Sharon and Skip always work as a team, channeling information from the dead among us. Sometimes they simultaneously receive information from the same spirit, while at other times they may tune into two or more different souls.

In one rare instance, Sharon saw a pair of ghosts just as Skip does. The strangers were standing on a curb outside of a Seattle area casino, while Sharon and Skip sat in their car nearby. Sharon did not notice anything unusual about them and she thought her husband was joking when he nudged her and said, "Do you see those people? They are dead."

Sharon laughed as she watched the middle-aged couple step off of the curb. They looked like normal folks, though they had absolutely no expression on their faces. They walked past the car and Sharon had to turn around in her seat to watch them go.

"When I turned around to look for them, they were gone!" she said.

Skip told me that the spirits had simply been hanging out at the casino because they had enjoyed the place in life. They were just two more ghosts passing by.

DONNA

Donna O'Dea was just six years old the first time a voice from the unknown spoke to her. "I was playing in the park," she remembered. "I was riding my imaginary horse. The wind was blowing through my hair and then I heard a male voice say, 'You will marry a man named Don.'"

The Sioux Falls, North Dakota, medium cannot tell me who the voice belonged to or why it spoke to her. She *can* tell me that the voice was right. She *did* marry a man named Don and had six children with him before they divorced.

She has received so many ethereal messages over the years that she can barely remember most of them. She simply passes them along to those who hire her for readings.

Donna "sees" with her mind's eye, and sketches the faces of the spirits who appear. She often experiences physical sensations when she tunes in. For instance, if she is channeling someone who died of lung cancer, she might have a coughing fit.

Donna sometimes receives calls from those in haunted places who are uncomfortable with the ghostly activity there. In one recent case, a salon owner from the historic section of downtown Sioux Falls requested her assistance. Unseen hands were turning the hair dryers on and off. "It frightened her," said Donna, who visited the salon on a December night in 2007, just after closing around 9:00 p.m. She brought several friends along, including Randi Hammers, a photographer, who often takes pictures of Donna in action. A new friend, Kathleen Rowland, also joined them.

The group entered the shop in a corner of an old brick building, and greeted the nervous operator. "I saw him right away," said Donna, who sees with her "mind's eye." The spirit sat in "the toenail chair," the seat used for pedicures. She sensed that the fellow was "sneering and belligerent" and knew that his name was George.

"They thought they killed me, but I escaped the penitentiary," the ghost said.

Donna instinctively knew that the man had been a killer who was executed in the electric chair, and she relayed the information to the group.

The medium believes that a bright light awaits even those who have behaved badly on earth, and that with prayers and encouragement, they can crossover to the Other Side.

"I always begin by praying that someone from the Other Side will come to help," she said. And as she made her request, another spirit appeared on the scene.

Donna turned to the others and said, "There is someone here named Ralph. He died from a wound to the head. He is here to help. Do any of you know a Ralph?"

Kathleen replied, "My uncle's name was Rapheal." The man had had ties to the mafia in Chicago and had given incriminating information to the police. When they found out, the mafia ordered a hit and he was shot in the head.

"He was murdered and he came to help a murderer," said Donna, who watched the two walk hand in hand into "the most beautiful light."

That evening, Randi began researching and found that only one person had ever been put to death in South Dakota's electric chair. His name was George.

He had shot a special agent who tried to arrest him and then escaped from prison while serving a life sentence for the murder. While on the run, he shot and killed Sheriff Dave Malcom on January 24, 1946.

He was strapped into the electric chair at age thirty-three on April 8, 1947. His last words were, "This is the first time authorities helped me escape prison."

When Donna heard the quote, she was positive that George Sitts was the same George she had met. He had told her that he had escaped from prison. Though he had apparently been joking when he made the remark before his execution, he was not trying to be funny when he spoke to Donna.

"He didn't know he was dead," she told me. "He thought that he was on the run."

She said the ghost had been "hiding out" in historic Sioux Falls, and going from building to building.

HOME SWEET HAUNTED HOME

Eleven-year-old Annie plopped down on her bed and kicked off her shoes. It was a winter night and snow fell outside the nineteenth-century Hillsdale, Michigan, home. Annie shivered, though it was not the frigid weather that sent a chill through her. It was the thing in her room. The thing in her *mirror*.

The mirror was attached to her antique dresser, which sat across the room from her bed. As Annie stared at the mirror, a bright ball of light began to form in the glass. She watched, fascinated as it took on a vague human shape.

"I can't see them very well," she told me. "But I can tell if it is a man or a woman. Usually it is the woman."

Ghost researcher Amy Williams had put me in touch with the family in the historic two-story home on the quiet, residential street. I had a conversation with the youngster about the people who appear in her mirror. The ghosts don't scare her. They have appeared so many times, she has grown used to them.

Amy, founder of the paranormal investigation group Haunted Hillsdale, has conducted several studies of the house. "We've found a number of unexplained cold spots and captured a photograph of a misty shape," she said.

Darla Winthrop* contacted Amy shortly after purchasing the old house when she realized that her daughter was seeing apparitions in her mirror. Amy agreed to investigate and quickly assembled her team. "The house had become run-down and dilapidated and Darla had restored the inside," Amy said. "She has beautiful antiques and hardwood floors. It is lovely, but there is something going on there. We noticed that the batteries on our equipment drained during the investigation. That happens frequently at haunted places."

Haunted Hillsdale team members visited for the first time on a dark, winter night and spent seven hours in the home. "We don't know what happened there to cause the haunting," Amy told me. "Others in the house have also had paranormal experiences. Darla has heard what sounds like a little boy playing on the stairs. And the family has heard the sound of something being dragged up and down the stairs."

Amy, who is making a documentary about the ghostly activity in the historic town, examined the artifacts found in the attic of the big house. "There were love letters to soldiers and locks of children's hair," she said, explaining that a study of the mementos may provide a clue about the people who once lived *and*, perhaps, died there.

Amy is not surprised that the ghosts manifest in the mirror. "Mirrors are portals to the Other Side," she said, adding that some people believe that closets also serve as passageways.

* Name changed to protect privacy.

No matter what entryway they choose, the ghosts are here among us. Some people report that the ghosts in their homes are *not* former residents, but people who once visited or had some sort of connection with the people who lived there, such as in the following story.

An English Tudor mansion in Loretto, Pennsylvania, was built by the family of railroad tycoon Henry Thaw, who made national news when he shot and killed a man in a jealous rage over his pretty wife, onetime Gibson girl, Evelyn Nesbit.

Former residents of the twenty-room mansion reported that Evelyn's ghost materialized in the hallway mirrors there, according to an October 27, 2001, edition of the *Post-Gazette*. Though Evelyn did not actually live in the house, she and Henry vacationed there in the early 1900s. They were known for the extravagant parties they hosted in the mansion. Despite the good times, Henry was obsessed with an incident in his pretty wife's past. Years earlier, at age sixteen, Evelyn had ended up in a compromising position with architect Stanford White when the older man got her drunk.

In 1906, Henry shot and killed Stanford on the roof of Madison Square Garden. He was eventually found not guilty by reason of insanity and sent to an asylum for a few years.

The mansion has since served as a restaurant, a church camp, and again as a private residence.

This historic postcard depicts Gibson girl Evelyn Nesbit Thaw whose ghost has been seen in the mirrors of the mansion where she once entertained. (author's collection)

Many believe that Evelyn's spirit is attracted to the place. She died in 1967 at age eighty-two and may be taking on the ghostly form of herself as she appeared during a happier time. In addition to manifesting in the mansion's mirrors, she is said to materialize in a long white dress by the side of Route 22 according to a newspaper account.

In undocumented cases, people offer rides to the beautiful, tearful lady who directs them to the gate of the mansion. Just before they reach the driveway, she vanishes from the car.

❧

Though encounters may be startling, and sometimes downright frightening, I've yet to meet anyone who suffered physical harm from a ghost. Read on for more stories of spirits in our homes.

VISITOR IN THE NIGHT

Sometimes it seems as if saltwater runs through the veins of those who live in the fishing villages that dot the rugged shores of Nova Scotia, Canada. When generation after generation makes their living from the sea, a love for the ocean is bred.

Mallory Arnott is no exception. The twenty-two-year-old student resides in Antigonish, and spends summers in the fishing community of Whitehead where her family owns a cottage on the beach.

In the summer of 2006, Mallory worked on a lobster boat. Her job as a researcher required her to count the crustaceans for a study on lobster population. Though she has seen it hundreds of times, she is always in awe as she gazes out across the shimmering waters of Tor

2/24/2021

BATES LISA MARIE

Item Number: 31901046097038

Contra Costa County Libraries are open for front door pick up of holds. Masks and social distancing are required. For faster service, book an appointment at: https://ccclib.org/front-door-service/ Book drops are available for returns. All Contra Costa County Libraries will be closed on February 15th. Items may be renewed online at http://ccclib.org, or by calling 1-800-984-4636, menu option 1. Pinole Library and Ygnacio Valley Library remain temporarily closed.

Hold Shelf Slip

Bay. Did the great-great-grandfather who built her family's cottage once marvel at the beauty of the bay as she does now?

Perhaps he did, though he was probably more concerned with feeding his family than enjoying the view. A fisherman's life is not an easy one, and it was especially hard on those who sailed a century ago, relying on winds and wits.

Mallory often finds herself wondering about past generations, especially when she visits the cottage. "It was built in the 1800s by my great-great-grandfather," she said.

Her great-grandmother Margaret had lived there as well. "She was born on August 27, 1886. *I* was born on August 27, 1986—*exactly* one century after her!" said Mallory, who finds the coincidence fascinating.

Margaret once lived in the cottage where Mallory spends her summers, looking out of the same windows that Margaret had as she watched the sea for a sign of her father's returning boat.

Did she inhabit the same upstairs room where Mallory sleeps? The doorways upstairs are surprisingly small. "I can barely fit through them and I'm five foot four. I guess people used to be shorter," she said.

Mallory was exhausted after one long day on the lobster boat. It was particularly dark that night as she climbed into bed and dropped off to sleep. She is not sure what woke her or how long she had been asleep when her eyes popped open. There, framed in the cramped doorway, was a stranger. He was a short man who easily fit in the little entryway.

"He was small, but he was *gruff* looking," she said. "He was wearing rain gear and a little hat. He was soaking wet, and he had pieces of seaweed on him as if he had come up from the ocean."

The image burned into her memory as she stared at him. "He wore a dark beard, and had piercing eyes that stared right into me. Then he started coming toward me, and I got so freaked out!"

Terrified, Mallory watched the dripping figure approach. Then, suddenly, he was gone, vanishing as quickly as a wave breaking upon the beach.

She could not budge from the bed. "I was too scared to move," she confided. "I just stared at the wall, and a light appeared on it in the shape of a window," she said, emphasizing that it was a moonless night and there was no logical source for the light. Her room faces the harbor, away from the road. The light could not have come from a car. When she finally got up the courage to peek out the window, she saw only blackness.

The bright square of light remained on the wall. As she watched, it grew brighter and then dimmed. "I wondered if it was my eyes playing a trick on me," she said. "Right before it disappeared, it got really bright and then it was gone."

The next morning, Mallory shivered when she remembered the strange encounter. Had she been dreaming? She considered the possibility. *No.* It was too real—too vivid—to have been a dream. When she told her mother and sister Melissa about the man, they barely paused before coming to a conclusion.

It was Reuben.

Reuben Munroe, Mallory's great-great-grandfather, had visited.

Of course! Of all the ghosts who would visit, Reuben was the most likely. He had built the cottage. He was father to Margaret, who had a kind of karmic connection to Mallory who was born exactly one century after her.

And Reuben had been lost at sea.

The apparition, dripping with bits of seaweed, indeed looked like the specter of a drowned sea captain emerging from the depths.

After encountering the ghost, Mallory searched newspaper archives for details. She was chilled by the account and more certain than ever that her great-great-grandfather had visited her ninety-six years after his death.

Tuesday morning, January 4, 1910, began as a cold but calm day. Fishermen from two Nova Scotia fishing villages were trawling for haddock when a blizzard swept down from the north. The snowstorm was so sudden that the men barely had time to react.

"Forty Fishermen of Dover and Whitehead, Swept to Sea by Fierce Blizzard, Still Missing" shouted the headline of the January 6, 1910, edition of the *Halifax Herald*.

Families kept vigil, praying that their men would come home again. The fishermen struggled to live as mountainous waves "threw the boats about like toys." At the end of the ordeal, those who survived were left with shredded sails and frostbite. It was a miracle that any of the men made it home—yet most of them did.

Only one crew did not return to Whitehead. The *Juanita*, with fifty-eight-year old Captain Reuben Munroe at the helm, was gone forever. The crew of two consisted of Reuben's son and his nephew. All three men were lost to the storm.

Mallory often ponders her encounter with the ghost from the sea. What was he doing in her room? Had it been his room at one time? Was he simply trying to go home to the safety and warmth of his bed? Was he angry or confused to find her asleep beneath his covers?

Several months after Mallory's encounter, her mother was sorting through family mementoes when she found old photographs of a man with a dark beard and intense eyes.

The photographs were not labeled, but Mallory recognized the man. "He is the man I saw," she said.

What about the window-shaped light, shining upon the wall?

"I concluded that it was the boat's light," she said, theorizing that the image was an apparition of the boat's light, shining one last time before the boat sunk.

LETTERS FROM
HAUNTED HOMES

My files are filled with letters from people who share their homes with ghosts. Some write to me for advice, others for reassurance that they are not crazy, and some just need to tell someone.

I am surprised by the number of people who feel that they have to convince me that they are sane before recounting their paranormal experiences. They are often embarrassed to admit to their encounters, and fear others will question their sanity.

"I grew up in a haunted house," I tell them, emphasizing that I have heard many ghost stories from credible people and that I, too, believe in ghosts.

In fact, it shocks me that so many people do *not* believe in ghosts. When I was a little girl, I figured that every home had a ghost just as it had a refrigerator. When I hear someone say that they don't believe in ghosts, it sounds as ludicrous to me as if they had said that they don't believe in refrigerators!

One lady prefaced her letter with the following: *I am a professional, functional, mentally well, stable person, but I believe in ghosts.* She went on to say that she works in law enforcement and then shared the following:

When my sister and I were growing up, unusual things occurred in our home. When I was a small child, I saw a shadowy shape in our garage. I thought it was a bear! The hallway of our home was built over the old footpath, on the land between my grandmother's and my great-grandmother's homes.

My mother had acquired the land between the two houses and built our house there. My sister often told us that she saw the ghost of a man in our house and once she saw him walking down the hallway, carrying a rope-handled bucket.

The man looked like my great-grandfather. My mother was his favorite grandchild and he had regularly walked the path between the two homes—the area that the hallway now occupies.

Sometimes, when I plugged my radio into an outlet in that hall, I would discover that it was turning itself on. My sister and I saw a heavy conch shell slide across the floor! And once in the kitchen, I saw a fork fly up and out of the drain board and into the sink.

The haunting she described makes perfect sense to me. Ghost researchers often note that apparitions are seen traveling a path that their live counterparts once walked in life.

Sometimes people write to me to share experiences that scared them. Lori was terrified by her encounter as a young wife in Lawton, Oklahoma, in 1977.

She wrote:

My husband was finishing up basic training in the army, so I was living in our apartment by myself for a couple of weeks. He had a few hours of leave when I first arrived and he got me a puppy to keep me company. That night I was alone and reading in bed when the puppy started whimpering. Then I heard the heavy footsteps of someone wearing boots.

At first I got excited because I thought that they had let my husband come home for the night. But then I remembered that I had locked the door and he did not have a set of keys! It sounded as if someone was walking around the kitchen. I threw a jacket on over my nightgown and ran out the living room door. I drove to the base and by the time I got inside my husband's platoon office I was incoherent and hysterical. I was convinced that someone had broken into the apartment.

Thank God my husband's commanding officer recognized me and had someone get my husband. My husband came home with me and we searched the apartment. We found no signs of forced entry. He thought that I was imagining things.

After that, sometimes when we were in the bedroom we heard footsteps in the living room. We also heard what sounded like someone sitting on our old, creaky couch. Often, the sounds continued all night long.

I woke up one night to see a shadowy figure beside the bed. I was too frightened to so much as nudge my husband—even with my arm right up against his side. After what seemed like hours, I fell asleep and when I woke up, it was gone.

We moved in with the couple downstairs after that night! We continued to hear the sound of footsteps and all kinds of noises coming from upstairs. After a particularly noisy day, we went upstairs to find that everything from the kitchen counter had been thrown on the floor.

Later, we learned that the apartments had once served as the army barracks for Fort Sill. I don't know who was haunting the place. Whoever it was, was not friendly.

Mark wrote to me about his spooky experiences in Celina, Texas:

It was in the late 1980s, and I was in the sixth grade. My mother and siblings and I moved into a rented home. It was a large, two-story home that was built in the 1800s. Though only four of us moved in, we all felt that there was a fifth presence in the house!

I was afraid to go inside when no one was home. On the rare occasion that I did, however, the hair on my neck stood up and I got the chills.

We had two working phones in the house that often rang and when we answered them, there was no one on the line. I know this could easily be explained away as calls from pranksters, but we had a third phone that also rang. It was an antique and not connected. It hung on the wall as a decoration!

One night I woke to the sound of a piano playing. All four of our bedrooms were upstairs, while my mom's baby grand piano was downstairs. I listened to the music for a few minutes before I woke up my family. We all heard the piano!

As soon as we went downstairs, the music stopped. We checked to make sure that the radio and stereo were turned off. We went back upstairs and the piano started playing again! We continued to go up and down the stairs and the pattern continued.

While Mark heard a musical spirit, Jeanette from Altoona, Pennsylvania, had to deal with the ghost of a barking dog. She wrote:

Our dalmatian, Lucky, passed away a few years ago on Christmas Eve. Since then, he has occasionally been seen barking in the front window. One day I was outside and saw neighborhood kids playing with their skateboards and doing jumps with their bikes. (Lucky had never liked this type of entertainment. He used to whine and jump up on me and my brother as if he was trying to stop us, whenever we got out our bikes to ride.)

The kids on the skateboard asked me if I could get the dog to stop barking. I told them that he didn't like bikes and skateboards, and then I walked up to our window and pounded on it and I yelled, "Shut up, Lucky!"

When I told the kids that my dog had been dead for a few years, they cleared out of there fast!

Not all ghostly encounters are frightening. Anna, a high school senior from Fremont, California, wrote to me about an experience that may have shocked her, but also touched her heart.

My great-aunt Jean, my great-grandma, and my grandpa all passed away within one year of each other. I was close with all of them and had been living with my grandparents. After my grandfather died, we moved to a smaller home.

Three months later, my friend and I were alone in my grandparents' former home, listening to the band, Evanscence.

Suddenly, the door to the hallway slammed shut. We were startled and immediately grabbed each other before getting up and slowly creeping toward the door. We peeked out and I looked down the hallway toward my grandparents' room. I could see into the room and was shocked to see my grandpa sitting on his side of the bed. He looked distraught, with his hands dangling in front of his knees. I called out to him and he looked up and smiled his amazing smile at me before he vanished.

I then proceeded to freak out and began to cry. I had just seen my grandfather and it was truly bittersweet. My friend had not seen him, but she believed that I had, for she has also seen spirits.

Ghosts

IN THE NEWS

Full House

The 2005 Halloween issue of the *Muskogee Phoenix* described ghostly encounters in an old home in Muskogee, Oklahoma.

The homeowners were only slightly surprised when acquaintances informed them that their house was mentioned on the annual Ghost Stories Caravan Tour hosted by the Three Rivers Museum.

Angelia Berryhill, a young mother of four, had moved into the home just five months prior and told journalist Keith Purtell about spirit activity in the house. "It's not scary," she told the reporter. "This house and this neighborhood are very peaceful. They are not going to harm us."

Berryhill confided that the ghost of a little girl had appeared at night at the top of the staircase. The child wore old-time garb, had brown hair, and clutched a doll.

Neighbor June Wood explained to the reporter that both the Berryhill house and her house had long ago served as quarters for mentally challenged children, and that she too, had seen the apparitions. One was the spirit of a little girl and the other was a man.

Tours are seasonal. For more information consult: cityofmuskogee.com

Tragic Lady

Residents of the former home of a convicted murderer reported seeing the ghost of an unidentified woman, according to the November 19, 2007, edition of the *Great Falls Tribune*. Journalist Kristen Cates interviewed occupants of the Great Falls, Montana, duplex where convicted wife killer Dennis Larson had lived in another house on the lot in the late 1970s.

Dennis Larson, while serving a sentence for the murder of his third wife, jumped from a prison window to his death. A second wife, Leslee Larson, went missing in 1975 but her body has never been found. Many suspect she was concealed somewhere on the property. Police searched the Great Falls home in the 1980s during an investigation into Leslee's death.

Kristen Cates recently investigated after tenants called the police when they discovered bones beneath their bathroom sink during renovation. She spoke to both past and current tenants of the house and learned that a number of people had reported seeing apparitions in the place that has long had a reputation as haunted.

From 1998 to 2002, eleven-year-old Malachi Dusek lived there with his family. He told the reporter that he had seen a woman in a white nightgown with a purse walking through the house. Once he had mistaken the ghost for his mother and followed her from room to room.

When the reporter spoke to eighteen-year-old Kristafer Lock, son of the current owners, he also spoke about sightings of a woman in white and said that the dress had a rose print.

The paper reported that a former landlord who owned the property in the 1980s noted that his tenants told him that they had seen a ghost there and that their dogs were afraid to go near the basement's dirt floor.

Author's note: As of this writing, police have yet to determine if the bones are human, though Kristen Cates told me that investigators suspect that the bones belong to an animal. The ghost seen on the property may be Leslee, or she may be a victim who went missing in the 1970s and has never been tied to Dennis Larson. Killers of his ilk have so much rage that they often count a number of victims, some who remain secret.

THE MYSTERY OF THE TRAVELING BISCUIT

Although many people e-mail me about their ghostly experiences, one in particular made me sit up and take notice. Phil Knight e-mailed me from his Austin, Texas, home. After explaining that he had heard me on a radio program, he wrote:

For a while we went through a time when objects would go missing, and then mysteriously show up again. The most startling occasion was a Saturday morning when I was making homemade biscuits for the family.

As I read Phil's words, I remembered an odd experience. Around 1995, I was taking a drive with a friend near Burien, Washington. As we rounded a corner, we were startled to see a biscuit rolling down a hill, on the side of the road. As it picked up speed, we followed it. It rolled along, unwavering, and we laughed because it made us think of the story of the runaway gingerbread boy.

We expected it to fall over, but strangely, it kept on going. I jumped out of the car and chased it. I plucked it from the road before it lost speed.

Where had it come from? We had seen no people or cars nearby. In a whimsical moment, I decided that it was a unique souvenir that I would save forever.

My friend had a trailer on his acreage near Mt. Rainier, and when we visited it later that day, we placed the runaway biscuit in a cupboard for safekeeping where I expected it to dry out and harden. I planned to shellac it to preserve it.

When I went to retrieve it a week or so later, it was gone.

I was disappointed. It was to be a silly conversation piece with a place of honor in my home. If boring guests were to visit, and the discussion dragged, I could whip out the biscuit and liven things up with the story of the runaway biscuit.

But the biscuit had vanished. I figured animals had gotten into the trailer and eaten it, though not a single crumb remained. The trailer windows had been shut, and the door locked. Perhaps it was a crafty mouse with a secret entrance, I thought, and did not ponder it much more.

It did not occur to me that anything paranormal had occurred, until I opened Phil Knight's e-mail. His letter continued:

I was at the stove, my wife was sitting at the dining table at the entrance to the kitchen, and there was a boy we were taking care of sitting at a little table in the kitchen with me, looking at a book.

I took the biscuits out of the oven, set them on the top of the stove, and then turned to the sink to do something. In a second or two, I turned back to the stove and there, in my nice pan of hot biscuits, on the side, was an empty place where one had been removed.

This occurred in a flash, and really startled me. I asked the boy if he had taken one of the biscuits, or whether he'd seen anybody come into the kitchen, and he looked up and said, "No."

I asked my wife if she had seen anyone come into the kitchen. She said no, that nobody had come in or left. I was left just scratching my head, wondering where that biscuit had gone, and whether ghosts like biscuits. We never found the biscuit.

I immediately sent Phil a reply. "I found your biscuit!" I told him.

Now, I realize that this sounds very strange so I will emphasize that I am not certain that the biscuits were one and the same. Yet, the two things were so weird and coincidental that I can't help exploring the idea.

In my e-mail, I told Phil of my biscuit experience and ended it by writing, "Life is strange. I know it's a stretch, but wouldn't it be something if your biscuit was somehow transported to where I found it?"

He responded, "Nothing would surprise me."

Phil and I cannot pinpoint the exact dates and times of our biscuit mysteries. When it comes to objects inexplicably transporting, however, time may not matter. Long before the biscuit incident, I had studied the phenomenon of objects transporting for one of my works of fiction, a novel with paranormal elements, and learned that items have been documented traveling through both space and time.

Was this the case with the biscuit? Though Phil and I had no connection when I found the biscuit, we have one now because we exchanged e-mails about the biscuit incident. It creates a mind-boggling circle.

Phil's biscuit mystery was fated to be mentioned in this book.

Where is the biscuit now? If one of my readers finds it, I hope they will let me know.